MANLY
MANNERS

for the

IMPECCABLE
GENT

GUY EGMONT

PLEXUS, LONDON

Address Book

NEW YORK

season

WOMAN

TOWN

WARDROBE

LIVING girls

CLOTHES

status

RESTAURANT

MEN CAREER

TOWN

LOOKS

COCKTAIL

SERVICE

gin fame

FASHION

GIRLS

WHITE-COLLAR

PRESENTS

MARRIAGE

LOVE

confidence

FOOD AND DRINK

FABULOUS

clothes

EXPENSE MEN

guests

eyes jewellery

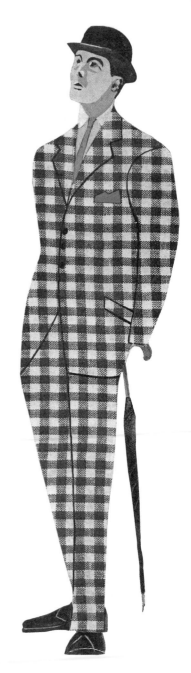

CONTENTS

1

EGMONT

AT

LARGE

NOTHING, THEY SAY, succeeds like success. Fair enough. But how do you start? What is the formula?

This is a question which has been asked down the ages, and, down the ages, it has always been fobbed off. Ask a millionaire and he will say facetiously either that he married a millionairess or that he was lucky (Bing Crosby, a multi-millionaire, entitled his autobiography *Call Me Lucky*) or that he genuinely worked eighteen hours a day from the age of twelve.

It is, of course, madness to deny that there are no short cuts to success. It is equally stupid to pretend that the same pattern is visible in the fortunes and careers of all rich men.

For, let us admit it right away, when we talk here of success we are talking about financial success, not about happy marriage, or being elected captain of your tennis club. Success, in fact, is self-expression at a profit. As the late Gilbert Harding was so anxious to point out, though, success primarily demands luck, a

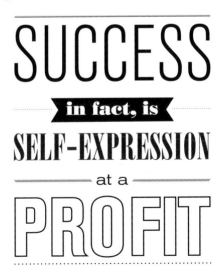

SUCCESS in fact, is SELF-EXPRESSION at a PROFIT

great deal of luck. Indeed, the greatest adjunct to success is the sheer good fortune of being in the right place at the right time. None of the Samuels or Clores of the 1960s could have become millionaires if they had not gone into the property market during or immediately after the Blitz.

But success demands more than good timing. It demands contacts, self-presentation, good manners, self-expression, sophistication, tact, concentration, the gentle art of flattery, of being a good guest and also of being a good host.

This manual is primarily devoted to teaching tact, how to make contacts, notes on social expertise, and to giving advice on what to avoid as unnecessary accomplishments or undesirable habits.

You must always be patient and unruffled, belong to one or two good clubs (the more the better), have a long memory, learn the latest gossip, never be unkind about anyone, acquire a ready smile but never a loud laugh, always pretend that the person to whom you are talking is, at the moment, the most enthralling person in the world, be able to make a really dry martini and discuss vintage years of clarets, burgundies, and champagnes with some show of authority, have a working knowledge of the French schools of painting, recognize good jewellery, gowns, and furs when you see them, always show interest in the photographs of other people's brats when confronted with them, but throughout all your debonair swanning never forgetting the main object of the exercise, which is almost invariably business-getting. Otherwise your accountants and fellow directors will take a very dim view of you.

There are several excellent pursuits ideally suited to the Egmonter at Large for their adaptability to his own ends in making contacts and business-getting; but some others are useless, except in special circumstances and with great virtuosity.

For example, to be good at lawn tennis is almost useless, as opposed to real tennis of which there are only about a dozen

ACQUIRE A READY
SMILE
BUT NEVER A LOUD
LAUGH
ALWAYS PRETEND
THAT THE
PERSON

to whom you are talking is at the moment

THE
MOST
ENTHRALLING PERSON
IN THE WORLD

courts in the country. Lawn tennis is a suburban sport practised by young men in the lower echelons of business. Quite true, if you were really good you might get a job with a sports outfitter. But that is presumably not your ambition, and it would seldom put you in touch with heads of big firms who might be looking for someone just like you.

Rugby football is a he-man's game and it certainly stood Sir Wavell Wakefield in good stead. The present chairman of the Scotch Whisky Association is also an ex-rugger international. No doubt one could find some dozens of ex-internationals, all very successful businessmen, who owed their start to success on the rugby field. But anything less than an international cap—such as a county cap—is not of much avail. In any event, like athletics and lawn tennis, it is a young man's game. You cannot take up rugger in the early thirties in order to make contacts.

The same applies to cricket. Playing for England has been a wonderful stepping stone for Peter May and his present career on Lloyd's, and you can certainly play cricket longer than you can play either code of football. If there were still the same amount of country-house cricket as there was before the war, it might indeed be recommended as a really useful password to business success.

Polo is frankly too expensive and limited in its clientèle. Squash racquets and real rackets are also young men's games.

We are left, therefore, with the most invaluable method of making contacts anywhere in the world this side of the Iron Curtain—GOLF. More business is initiated on golf courses such as Sunningdale, Walton Heath, Formby, Ganton, Addington, Wentworth, and the major golf courses in Scotland, than in any club, restaurant, or hotel.

You are with your contact for three to eight hours at a time, away from the telephone—*most* important—with a break for luncheon and the attendant drinks. Possibly, too, with the drive down and back.

It is a game which you can take up quite late in life, but the earlier the better so that you can acquire a low handicap and, when necessary, play a customer's game—allowing your opponent to win or halve at the last hole, or earlier, if you prefer it. You will find that most of the important people you want to meet have started playing regularly after they had made their money and so are likely to have long handicaps. They are also likely to be real addicts, talking their heads off about their new hobby. By being sympathetic and helpful in the locker-room or on the course, you can get on intimate business terms which would take years to achieve in the office or boardroom. Every young man who aspires to business success must, in our opinion, learn golf and play it well enough to be truly handicappable. That is to say, to be allotted a handicap of not more than 18 and preferably less than 10. It was the late Lord Hore-Belisha who once said to us 'all interesting men have long handicaps'. By which he meant that all really successful men in his day had taken up golf in middle age.

Golf is the only game in which trade matches, competitions and tournaments regularly take place—with the exception of the annual cricket match between the Authors and Publishers. Every really big firm, profession, and industry has its own golfing society and golf fixtures, whether it be the N.A.G.S. (Newspaper and Advertisers Golfing Society), the Bar Golfing Society, the Parliamentary Golfing Society, or those of the Toy Manufacturers, Haulage Contractors, W. H. Smith's, Chartered Surveyors, Westminster Bank, or anyone else.

Apart from observing the usual rules of etiquette, never announce gaily, when you have misguidedly beaten someone by 7 and 6, that you won by a dog licence. You will never be forgiven.

Always be punctual for a competition or team match. In the

latter case, if you have won by a revoltingly large margin, it is polite to mark it 'one up' on the board.

If in a four-ball you notice that there is a very important chap playing along behind you in another match, invite him and his party to go through. Whether or not he accepts, and however the rest of your own party may protest, it earns you splendid marks.

It is very mean to have your name or initials stamped on your golf-balls. Its end result is that if you lose one and it is found, it has to be returned to you.

If you are playing for more than a ball, which we hope you are, let the other chap name the sum. If it is still very small and you think you can beat him, you can always say with a laugh, 'I'll bet you the same that you've made a bad bet.' If he accepts it, you've doubled the stake without pressing him unduly.

If you are playing a customer's game and he misses his first tee shot, say 'I always play Mulligans, don't you? Have another.' A Mulligan is a free extra tee shot, but only on the first tee, an idea imported from the U.S. You can also give him three-foot putts, but don't overdo it with a five-footer. He might become suspicious.

Always help an opponent look for a lost ball. It is surprising how many people merely send their caddies over to help nowadays.

If you lose, it is always a good thing to hand over the stake to your opponent as you walk off the course and before you reach the club house. Always commiserate politely with your opponent if you win. Never curse what may be your genuinely bad luck if you lose. Being a member of the Two Club and paying sixpence for a 2 is suburban, but agree if it is suggested to you.

If you are presenting a cup for a new competition, think about a weight-for-age event. In this, each player subtracts his handicap and age from his gross score. Thus, a man of 60 with a handicap of 8 who goes round in 82 returns a card of 14, whereas a youngster of 26, who is scratch and goes round in 72, returns a card of 46. Older players have every chance of winning and it is the older players who are likely to be more practical in their appreciation of you.

Remember to double your stakes whenever you play someone who has just had a lesson. You are sure to win.

Racing is another method of making contacts. It is, of course, very expensive, and people you meet are much too interested in the horses to pay any real attention to you. One inviolable rule at a race meeting is never to volunteer a tip, however sure you are that your animal—I mean the one in which you have confidence—is going to win. The chances are that it will not, and you have lost a friend. If anyone 'gives' you a horse and it wins, thank him profusely and assure him that you backed it heavily, whether or not you had anything on it.

Incidentally, it is a status symbol to have a bookmaker, even if you always ask him for Tote odds. Never bet on the Tote. It lowers

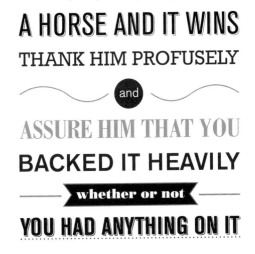

............*If anyone 'gives' you*............

A HORSE AND IT WINS

THANK HIM PROFUSELY

and

ASSURE HIM THAT YOU

BACKED IT HEAVILY

whether or not

YOU HAD ANYTHING ON IT

your prestige enormously, though Tote Investors are O.K., and always say you have had a winning day or 'haven't done so badly'. Never admit to losing, not even 'a packet', unless you do it with a bright smile suggesting that it is a mere bagatelle.

As for indoor games, the aspirant to success must be able to play a decent game of bridge, which in the old days was almost as useful as golf for making contacts, whether in the club or the home. It is easy enough to take lessons in the evening instead of watching the goggle-box, and certainly less expensive than learning golf—which, however, remains a *sine qua non*. If you can trouble to learn gin-rummy, piquet, 4-pack bezique, backgammon, and canasta as well, so much the better. Canasta is a middle-aged woman's game, but if your boss's wife likes it, so much the better. Never admit to playing solo, cribbage, whist, or hearts, even if you can. As Wykehamists would say, they are *Infra Dig*.

Another excellent way of making contacts is, of course, 'swanning' on the Continent. Rich men are much more likely to unbutton their reserve in the heady atmosphere of casino towns like Cannes and Monte Carlo and other foreign resorts, sunbathing, golfing, watching the gamblers. Really rich men never gamble themselves, except at the cheapest tables and then only for a few minutes of relaxation. Being rich, they know that the odds are stacked against them when they can see that each roulette table supports a minimum of six employees of the casino.

But however you go about making your contacts, remember that you must never 'chase' anyone in business.

The code of honour of the Egmont at Large must be quite as strict as that of the knight errant of more chivalrous days. It should, however, be up to the minute in style, and be designed to present him to the greatest possible advantage to his contacts.

Good self-presentation—what the advertising fraternity call

creating an image—is vital. It begins with your teeth, hands, and hair, in that order.

We know at least two assistant-executives who would be managing directors if they had been to their dentists and had their discoloured fangs fixed. A pleasant smile is impossible with bad teeth, and yet it must be worth at least a couple of thousand pounds a year to a highly-placed account executive in a top advertising agency. One agency is said to be so short of pleasant smiles that it actually employs an actor to sell its sales promotion schemes to new clients.

The hands of the aspiring millionaire need to be manicured at least once a month. And at all costs, they must show no signs of nicotine on the fingers. Nothing is more revolting to a woman or more tell-tale to a would-be employer. Over-smoking means nerves and probably a bad digestion. What is the matter with pumice-stone or even a small cigarette holder? Filter-tips help, too.

You cannot help the shape of your hands. But at least let them be clean, particularly the nails. This is no easy matter if you work in a big city, but it is essential to create a good impression on your contacts.

Hair is not quite so important as the advertisements suggest. But you really should be well-groomed on top. This is proved more and more by television close-ups and it applies to moustaches as well. Mr Harold Macmillan, when Foreign Secretary, had a straggly moustache and untidy hair. Now, thanks to Henry Manton, his barber at Topper's, he is as soigné as any film star, and much more so than the average duke. Sidewhiskers, particularly on a lean face, are somehow untrustworthy. Handle-bar moustaches show the extrovert or suggest an inferiority complex. As for beards, it is a phenomenon of English history that whenever the monarch is a queen, there is always a tendency to beards. In the case of a young man who knows he has a weak chin, it is not a bad

SIDEWHISKERS

PARTICULARLY ON A LEAN FACE

ARE SOMEHOW

UNTRUSTWORTHY ...

HANDLE-BAR MOUSTACHES

show the

EXTROVERT

OR SUGGEST AN

INFERIORITY COMPLEX

thing to grow a small well-kept beard, particularly if he is in the commercial art world. But a straggly beard, and many men cannot grow a good one, is even worse than a straggly moustache. The very thin hair-line moustache should also be avoided. It is neither one thing nor the other and, on the whole, rather irritating. It suggests a small mind, a natty character.

Never carry a comb with you.

Clothes come next. A good wardrobe is obviously important. So are hats. If possible, afford a hat from one of the top shops, like Lock. You may be able to conceal the fact that you have bought your suits ready-made. But you take off your hat and leave it on a peg or a chair or in a cloakroom so often in the course of the week that people are bound to know whether it is a cheap one or not. Besides, it is an economy. A good hat lasts years longer and comes up like new whenever it is cleaned.

Ties and shirts are practically a chapter in their own right. If you are entitled to wear what is generically known as an Old School Tie, whether it represents your public school, university, regiment, golf club, rowing club, or any other sporting or social associations, wear it sparingly. The Old Etonian who always flaunts the pale blue stripe on the black background is either a snob or unsure of himself. This holds good with any school or even the Brigade of Guards, though to a lesser degree in the latter case.

The average well-dressed man has probably at least a couple of dozen ties of which six are representative ties. These should be worn only for special occasions, except perhaps if travelling on the Continent, when a well-known tie can often lead to useful conversations.

Bow ties, suspect a few years ago as a sign of degeneracy, are now coming back to fashion and look very well on small men, provided they are properly tied. Heaven help the man, incidentally, who is ever caught wearing a ready-made bow tie.

Shirts should be plain and the collars should be detachable in business hours. A stiff white collar is much smarter than a soft one and remember that you should never wear a bowler hat with a soft collar, any more than you could possibly wear a bowler hat with brown shoes. The trouble with the stiff collar is that its points are inclined to fray the shirt after quite a short time, and a frayed shirt is as bad as a frayed cuff or frayed turn-ups. They all immediately inspire doubt about your financial status and the tidiness of your mind. It is surprising how many managing directors study the shirts and cuffs of applicants for jobs.

Never wear a wing collar except with a white tie, and never wear a soft shirt with it.

Never wear a bowler hat without carrying an umbrella and never carry an umbrella if you are not wearing a hat. It is quite out-of-date, meaningless, and was never really smart. Never wear your bowler hat, or indeed any hat, on the back of your head.

Shoes? If you can afford them initially, hand made shoes from people like Lobb are an economy. They last two or three times as long. They are also a real status symbol, more so even than a Brigg umbrella. Always remember in the latter reference that the ferrule of your umbrella must be of wood and not of metal.

Opinions differ on suede shoes. They used to be regarded as somewhat effeminate. But today, particularly on a large man, they are perfectly proper in our opinion, unless they are black, in which case they may be thought to be slightly la-di-da.

There is much to be said for a smoking jacket in the house for informal dinner parties—bottle-green or maroon, but never Cambridge blue.

Platinum watch chains and key chains, popularized by the late Michael Arlen, are chi-chi unless worn with full evening dress. Signet rings are fine if you come of an armigerous family, but ***not*** otherwise.

Never show your braces in any circumstances. If you are going to play snooker, remove them simultaneously with your jacket, unless you are wearing a waistcoat.

Never use those small blue plastic hold-alls given to you by most air lines. It is very bad form.

Never carry a fountain pen visibly in your breast pocket. A cigar case is different, but this should be largely obscured by the handkerchief.

There is a very great deal to be said for carrying a cigarette case. It is almost a 'must', but never made in leather, unless it contains at least twenty cigarettes or has sentimental value. Indeed, the only excuse for not having one is if you smoke king-size cigarettes which do not fit easily into either a gold or a silver case. But, if yours is gold, do not be too ostentatious about it. Americans, by the by, practically never carry them. Odd.

Few rich men wear wedding rings.

If you wear spectacles, let them be neat and not gaudy. If you are still young, do not wear very heavy ones. It looks as though you are trying to appear to be much more important than you are. As a status symbol, they should be real tortoiseshell, although tortoiseshell cracks very easily and is wildly expensive. Never wear steel spectacles. The choice of shape depends a great deal on your own face. Fleur Cowles' face is absolutely made by her spectacles, if it is not ungallant to say so. Don't wear dark glasses unnecessarily, unless you are a short-sighted woman who can have special lenses put in them to conceal her disability, and, after all, you are not a woman. Everything here is addressed to men.

So much for physical and sartorial self-presentation.

Another all important problem is that of your christian name and surname. There is nothing, of course, to prevent you altering your surname by law, but it needs to be done while you are comparatively young and unknown. What you can do is to decide which of your christian names has the more imposing sound in business.

Nearly everybody has more than one.

Choose the more unusual one (it may be your mother's maiden name). There are thousands of John Clarkes and Bill Smiths and Harry Browns. Russell Clarke, Robinson Smith or Wilson Brown will be far more easily remembered. Above all, never use an initial before or after your christian name. George A. White or Dennis L. Watson or F. Robert Green is a sign of mediocrity. Use one christian name only. Of course, there are the exceptions which prove the rule like J. Walter Thompson or Ethel M. Dell or Alan B. Fairley. But if both your christian names are weak, like Percy or Albert, it is far better to be known by your initials, as you probably will be, anyway, when you become the boss of the firm. Perhaps the most brilliant transmogrification in recent years was that of Dick Hands to Richard Lonsdale-Hands, the industrial designer. Richard Lonsdale-Hands conjures up a tycoon.

Private addresses in London before the war were exceedingly important, both from the point of view of business and social standing. Mayfair and Knightsbridge and the squares such as Bryanston Square, Montagu Square and Portman Square, were a hallmark of importance, unless you lived in a mews off them. Good-bye to all that.

Kensington, once frowned on, is as smart as Belgravia. Today, it does not really matter where you live—Chelsea, Islington, Bloomsbury, St John's Wood, Bayswater, or the outer suburbs such as Harrow, Putney, or Croydon. Wimbledon, indeed, is becoming positively fashionable. There are, however, a few areas in which it is not permissible to live, unless you should have a house of exceptional historical or architectural beauty.

On the whole, there is a tendency nowadays to spend far too much money on your rent in proportion to the rest of your income. There is less and less real entertaining in the home, except among the very well-to-do. At the same time, it must be tolerably well-furnished and never over furnished.

Incidentally, the actual address of your bank is more important than your own. If you bank as a private individual at Head Office it is very much better than in some suburban branch. It may be tough on the bank manager who looked after you so well in your early years, but if you are to be successful, you must take this into consideration.

Don't forget that the most successful men are always the most punctual, just as punctuality is the politeness of princes and the courtesy of kings.

Never be late for an appointment, but equally do not arrive too early. It makes you look anxious. The only exception to the rule is in Ireland, where you are within your rights to be half an hour late or early. In Ireland, they refuse to be the slave of time. They kick it around.

Always rise when a woman comes into a room. In a restaurant, when a passing woman bows to you, make the gesture of rising by half-standing up and bowing back, then sit down again.

NEVER

—— BE LATE FOR ——
AN APPOINTMENT
—— *but equally do not* ——
ARRIVE TOO EARLY
—— IT MAKES YOU LOOK ——
ANXIOUS

Always take off your hat if a woman is present in a lift belonging to a block of flats, private house, or hotel. But it is quite unnecessary to do so in a department store lift. Always take your hat off to a woman whom you know if you meet in the street. Don't just tip it. At Ascot, you take it off and bring down below the level of your head. If you pass a woman in a narrow space, lift your hat.

Always walk on the side nearest to the road when you are escorting a woman. See that she goes out through the swing doors ahead of you, even if you have to give them a preliminary push. In this age of emancipation it depends very much, we are afraid, on the beauty or the age of a woman whether you offer her your seat in the rush hour on the Underground.

Stand straight up, arms to the side, quite motionless, when the National Anthem is played in a cinema, theatre, or any other public place. Don't fidget, and above all, do not move towards the exit while it is still being played. It is insufferable bad manners.

When the Loyal Toast is given, just say 'The Queen'. Never add 'God bless her'. And it is perfectly proper when the National Anthem is sung not to join in the words. Once again, you just say 'The Queen' when it is over.

Always take your hat off if the Queen's Colour is being carried by a detachment of troops.

Walking along with your hands behind your back was always very correct, but never walk out of doors with your hands in your pockets.

Never be seen on television smoking a cigarette. Make it a cigar or nothing. When being photographed by a studio photographer, never let him take you with your chin on your hand. It suggests that you have a weak one.

Never have your own photograph in your own sitting-room or office.

Do not keep out-of-date invitations on your mantelpiece.

Besides having a bookmaker, other status symbols are your own bespoke tailor, your top West-End barber, your own wine merchant (not a store), and half a dozen restaurants where the head waiter knows you by name. A barman who knows you too well may have a boomerang effect. It may suggest that you go there too often.

Reverting to golf, nothing is better than to have your own caddy or series of caddies instead of being a 'barrow-boy'. But you should never go out of your way to recommend your own dentist, doctor, chartered accountant, stockbroker, or lawyer to other people, unless you are specifically asked to do so.

A status symbol which can be embarrassing is to have a personalized number-plate for your motor-car. It all began with the late Harry Tate, who secured the number-plate T8. In those early days of only one or two letters of the alphabet being used, it was the Lord Lieutenants of the various counties who were entitled to the numeral 1. Later Lord Brabazon of Tara secured FLY 1 and Brigadier General A. C. Critchley acquired all the numbers from 1 to 36 of GRA (a Derby number plate) for himself and his Greyhound Racing Association directors and associates.

Today, most ambassadors and High Commissioners have secured the premier number of the letters of the alphabet most suitable for them—such as USA 1 and NZ 1. Since, like Caesar's wife, they are automatically above reproach in their public outings, it is good publicity and also useful for the traffic police. But, we repeat, and we know, it can sometimes be embarrassing to have a well-known number-plate followed by the numeral 1. Even Cary Grant discovered this. Nevertheless, many big business-men like to have their initials represented on their motor-cars. So many do it, indeed, that it is ceasing to be smart in either sense of the word.

A Rolls-Royce will always be a status symbol, particularly if the chassis is an estate car or a taxicab.

Your own personal book matches are also quite good fun.

It is good to recognize some of the better known 'old school ties': Old Etonian, Old Harrovian, Old Carthusian, Old Wykehamist, Old Rugbeian, M.C.C., Savage (best known of all on television), Garrick, Lords Taverners, the R. and A., Leander, Hawks, Vincents, Rifle Brigade, and the like. It is, incidentally, one of the curiosities of 'old school ties' that in 95 per cent of them, the stripes go left to right. Striped ties which go right to left are usually foreign and therefore pretty safe to buy if you like the colours; though effigy ties are much smarter.

If you are compelled to give a business cocktail party which includes the Press, make it a *champagne d'honneur*. You serve nothing but champagne and occasional soft drinks for teetotallers. But no whisky and no gin and no brandy. It sounds smarter, *is* smarter, costs less and avoids any risk of your guests getting tight. On such occasions, if you have provided the Press with a hand-out, for goodness sake don't read it out loud to them. Just welcome them, refer briefly to the hand-out, and let them go on drinking again. Always have at least one flashlight photographer and, if possible, a ciné-camera man as well. Whether or not there is any chance of it being seen on television, it makes everybody feel very important.

If you are on an expense sheet basis, remember that the word 'towards' is the most valuable in the whole language. For if you arrange that you are paid a fixed sum of X pounds 'towards' expenses, it presumes automatically that this figure does not fully cover them and your accountant can recover a certain amount.

Never talk crudely about money, particularly about what your own things cost or the price of your holiday abroad.

Never talk with your hand over your mouth, unless you do not wish to be heard.

Never talk disparagingly about the United States. Americans are very sensitive and it may always get back to the wrong person, just when you are wanting to do a deal.

NEVER TALK DISPARAGINGLY *about the* UNITED STATES AMERICANS ARE VERY SENSITIVE and it may ALWAYS GET BACK TO THE WRONG PERSON JUST WHEN YOU ARE WANTING *to do a* DEAL

Interrupt as seldom as possible. If you must do so, give some mild signal by half raising your hand.

If you are ever forced into passing an opinion on someone truly detestable, it is always wiser to say 'He's a strange fellow', and leave it at that.

Never carry a chip on your shoulder. It has ruined dozens of otherwise successful men.

In no circumstances, use the phrases 'U' or 'Non-U'.

Never get the reputation for creating bad blood inside the office. It will ruin you.

Never use a toothpick in public.

By rights you should not have your telephone number on your visiting card. But this rule is observed more in its breach than in its practice.

If you think of buying a house in the country, stay at least two nights in the neighbourhood to make sure there is no military airfield in audible distance and that it is not in a direct line of civilian aircraft passing overhead.

Don't dye your hair with pomade as you become older. Nobody will believe that it is really natural when you are past sixty. Besides, your face won't fit it.

A clever way of carrying a single cigar is in the upturn of your socks. It never crumbles. Try it sometime.

Distrust any man who maintains his military rank, such as Major or Colonel, although he never went to Sandhurst or 'the Shop'. There must be something wrong somewhere.

A social club is naturally a most important asset, as essential as golf. A club-less man is sure to be regarded with some misgiving. Was he blackballed? Doesn't he know anyone to put him up? Has he B.O.? Isn't he popular?

The advantages of a social club are not only that you make new contacts, but also that you can entertain a guest in a place which is metaphorically out-of-bounds to him. Incidentally, if you exclude the entrance fee and annual subscription, which your firm may pay for you, the cost of meals and wines is usually less

A SOCIAL CLUB

IS NATURALLY A MOST IMPORTANT

ASSET

—————— *as essential as* ——————

GOLF

A CLUB-LESS MAN

—————— is sure to be ——————

REGARDED WITH SOME MISGIVING

than in a restaurant. But your first few visits to your club must be exceedingly circumspect. Don't make an appearance for at least three weeks after your election. And even then, you must come, if possible, with your sponsors, to whom you give luncheon or dinner as a matter of course. After which you should still make only sporadic appearances for another three months. Never offer to join an older member. Make friends with the club stewards and find out whether, by protocol, certain armchairs and tables are unofficially reserved for certain oldsters. Never offer to stand a round of drinks at the bar to people you don't know, and be particularly careful whom you bring as guests. A club member is always liable to be judged by the company he keeps and the people he brings along.

If there happens to be a card room or a snooker room, wait until you are asked to play. Never volunteer. Discover who the club bores are. There are always two or three.

Never raise your voice. Wait for people to come to you. They always will—particularly if your first few guests are in any way distinguished. Never appear during bank holidays, if the club

DISCOVER
WHO THE
CLUB BORES
are

There are always

TWO OR THREE

happens to be open. It will mean to those who see you that you've nowhere better to go, which is bound to be true of them, so they are of no practical use to you anyway. Always call a much older man 'Sir', and you can always throw a 'Sir' to a younger one if you want him to pass the salt or perform some minor courtesy for you.

Be an attentive listener. If anyone tells you an allegedly funny story which you've heard before, never interrupt, even if he says 'stop me if you know it'. Laugh politely anyway. And don't try immediately to cap it with what is undoubtedly a better one on the same subject.

Equally, if someone mentions a person or a place or a fact which is new to you, don't pretend you are a know-all and that it is old-hat so far as you are concerned. Nothing is more infuriating than to have someone say 'Yup. Yup. Yes, I know', particularly when it is evident that he could not possibly do so. Arrogance, an air of superiority (often based on an inferiority complex) and any form of sarcasm is the kiss of death to the man who wants to succeed.

One of the most popular but most useless forms of making contacts is going to cocktail parties. These are usually boring, with more women than men, with slightly warm and, therefore, more intoxicating drinks, starting at about half past six, in the middle of the rush-hour, with completely idle conversation and no major effort from the average host or hostess to give the names audibly of the people to whom you are introduced. Little or no business emerges from cocktail parties.

THE IMPORTANCE OF a likeable wife cannot be exaggerated in the world of business. If you are not yet married, remember that the American habit of big firms screening executives' wives before possible promotion is spreading to this country.

If your wife has a private income, it is a tremendous advantage. There is much less likelihood of your being pushed around or fired. Once your boss knows that you are independent, he will cosset you, if you are any good at all.

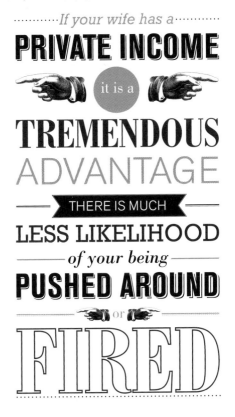

If you are already married, you must make up your mind whether you treat your wife as part of the marriage team, take her into your confidence and ask her advice, or whether you treat her as a decorative (we hope) hostess, who has no head for business and is primarily the mother of your children and your unpaid housekeeper.

Your choice should inevitably be dependent on her character. But in either event, it is essential that she gets on well with the wives of your business associates, quite apart from the husbands. She must train herself to listen sympathetically to all their operations, domestic problems, flirtations (if any), the brilliance of their children, their holiday plans, and the backslidings of their husbands. She must show no sign of distress if you bring back guests unexpectedly to dinner. She must never interrupt your stories, however often she has heard them. She must learn enough about bridge to be able to play a hand when required. She must never quarrel with you in front of the guests, whatever she may say to you as soon as they have gone.

Perhaps the best way to deal with the whole subject is to put it on a profit and loss basis.

Is she healthy? Is she an invalid?

Is she rich or the reverse?

Is she tactful or not?

Is she an only child or have you dozens of in-laws? Has she dress sense? Is she extravagant?

Is she a chain-smoker? Can she cook?

Does she play golf? And so on.

Like her husband, Egmont's wife must be subject to the same rigorous training and discipline.

If she is at all plump, never let her wear white. Remember that if she is going to be properly dressed either by day or in the evening, she should carry either suede or kid gloves—never

IF SHE IS

at all

PLUMP

NEVER LET HER WEAR

WHITE

anything man-made or fabric. Short gloves are not smart with evening dress. They ought to go more or less up to the shoulder.

If you have stalls at the opera, do not let her wear her biggest and most bunchy dress. It is hell for everybody, including herself.

Make sure she buys some good costume jewellery. Remember that Fisher fur is very smart and also hardwearing. Most of it, alas, is exported to France. If she wants mink, tell her truthfully that it is not at all as smart, indeed rather vulgar, but that white fox is back in fashion. If she wants mutation furs, tell her that they remind you of old women who dye their hair. That ought to fix it. If she insists on sable, you've had it.

Remember, too, that if you are in anything like a big way of business, your accountant should be able to secure you at least £200 or £300 a year allowance for your wife's clothes, in so far as she is your hostess and has to be dressed better than other women to promote your business interests.

Stockbrokers, of course, are not included in the above paragraph, as they know only too well.

If she knows nothing about wines, try to educate her up to the standard of enjoying a red wine and never wanting a sweet white one.

HER **DISCOURAGE** FROM **TELEPHONING** UNLESS **THE** *you at the office* MATTER IS **VITAL**

Discourage her from telephoning you at the office unless the matter is vital.

If she plays golf, discourage her from wanting to play with you except in some annual mixed foursome competition, and insist that she wears gloves on both hands.

If you are dubious about her discretion, have a bet with her that she cannot keep a secret and then tell her some fascinating gossip about one of her closest acquaintances and see whether she 'leaks' it within the next four days.

Never let her wear slacks unless she has boyish hips.

If you have no children, persuade her to take up some hobby, such as petit-point or gros-point.

Never let her gossip with the staff when she is having a treatment at her hairdresser's. We have always suspected that some of the snoop columns pay well for indiscretions.

The whole art of being well-bred in these surroundings is to be on very friendly, but not gossipy terms. Your wife will have her own special girl assistant, whom she will learn to call by her christian name. But no woman of any dignity will be on familiar terms with her hairdresser if he is a man. Men hairdressers are usually young and temperamental, inclined to be impertinent with a new client if they think they can get away with it. If a woman is at all unsure of herself, she is wide open to being bullied by her hairdresser. If, of course, she is regularly unpunctual, she must expect some discourtesy. But if although she is consistently punctual and tips reasonably well, her hairdresser shows any sign of temperament, she should just leave at the end of the treatment and never come back. She should never have a tiff with him on the spot. If only certain women knew how they are laughed at behind their backs, they would think twice about making fools of themselves by complaining unreasonably each time they have their hair done—and then continue to come back.

Never let your wife speak of a beauty parlour as such. If she has had a treatment at her hairdressers, well that is what she has had, not a facial.

If she has had her hair shampooed and set, she has had her hair done. No more, no less.

In short, Egmont's wife must, indeed, be above suspicion.

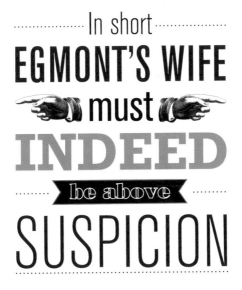

In short
EGMONT'S WIFE
must
INDEED
be above
SUSPICION

3

EGMONT

THE

URBANE

FLATTERY, THEY SAY, will get you nowhere. Nonsense. It is one of the shortest cuts to success if the slightest delicacy is used. In the case of a big business-man, you have almost endless opportunities of endearing yourself to him by flattering him openly or behind his back, knowing that it will filter back to him through his secretary or someone. I once landed a splendid job by letting a millionaire know that I thought he had 'very fine hands'. Mind you, he had. (There has to be a modicum of truth in most flattery.) The fact that he was self-made added to the value of the remark.

Obviously you can't flatter any self-respecting man on his sheer looks, although there is no harm in asking him where he gets his hair cut, which, by inference, suggests that you admire it. On the other hand, there is an absolute surefire way of winning him if he is sufficiently important to appear on television in some interview or panel or other serious programme. It does not matter how awkward, humming and hawing, dull, unphotogenic or even ignorant he proved to be, just drop him a line and say how good he was. He will be delighted, even though he knew he was a flop.

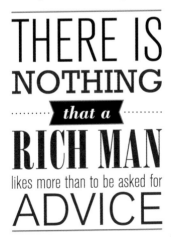

THERE IS NOTHING *that a* RICH MAN likes more than to be asked for ADVICE

You can flatter him about his clothes and shoes in the same way as his hair. Ask him where he gets them. That goes for ties as well. It suggests that he is a man of taste and that you appreciate it and would like to find out for yourself.

There is nothing that a rich man likes more than to be asked for advice. Never, if you can help it, ask a millionaire for a job. Ask for advice, and he will very probably see you. Ask for a job and there is a barrier of secretaries and lower-echelon members of his staff between you and the great man.

It is usually safe to flatter him on his children and on the appearance of his wife. But it is safer still to flatter the wife about them and herself.

Never run anyone down, particularly your own relations. (We refuse to use that very second-rate word 'denigrate' which is now so popular.)

Nothing is worse than to downcry a rival or someone whose job you want in front of a third person. Always be jolly decent about them, unless they are so painfully inefficient that it would look as if you had absolutely no sense of judgment yourself in lauding them. There is, of course, the art of 'damning by faint praise', but it must be desperately subtle. Most people in business have some quality or other which has kept them in their job. Praise that one and let all his failures go by default.

Wherever possible agree with the man from whom you want something, at least at the beginning of the interview. Later on, you may be able to work round to a perfectly different tack and persuade him to disagree with himself. And if any bright idea emerges from your conversation, make it seem on leaving that it was his thought and not yours. Platitudinous? Maybe. But how it works! When you are trying it out the first time, it is not a bad gambit to say, 'I really forget who brought it up, but that is certainly worth thinking about.'

THE FACT REMAINS
that what would have been
REGARDED AS
'SMARMY'
in the past is now
SWALLOWED WITHOUT A
BLUSH

It is astonishing how much flattery can be absorbed by the other person if you do it really well. Perhaps it is because of the hard years of the war and just afterwards, when everything was damnable. The fact remains that what would have been regarded as 'smarmy' in the past is now swallowed without a blush.

The ways to flatter a woman, whether she is the secretary or the wife of the millionaire you want to impress, can take many forms. In the case of the secretary, you flatter her on her discretion, sense of humour, the way she deals with people over the telephone, her voice, and her tact. Where possible find out her interests in life— ballet, theatre, tennis, holidays abroad. The great thing is to make her realize that you are treating her as a human being and not as a wage-slave. Personal private secretaries wield an immense power. Their study can reap rich rewards. It is not just a question of sending them a bottle of perfume at Christmas, or a couple of theatre tickets, or even flowers. It is a matter of asking after their family, occasionally commiserating with them over the late hours they keep at the office.

In the case of the wife, if she has children she will be much more ready to talk about her sons than her daughters. If you know anything about the schools or universities at which they are, so much the better. Be very careful about flattering her on looks or clothes. On the other hand, you can be very lavish in your praise of her daughter's appearance. No mother will resent it.

If you are dining at her home, don't compliment her in general terms on her food. But if there is one particular dish you liked, say that it is one of your favourites.

Notice whether she is the fussy type. When there is not a thing out of place, her eyes will flicker with anxiety whenever a cigarette is lighted for fear the ash will be dropped somewhere other than in the ash tray. Be very careful about your cocktail or liqueur glass. It can so easily leave a mark on the patina of a well polished table when there is the slightest moisture on the base. If you say, 'I hate to put this down on your beautiful table,' you will really have endeared yourself to her, even though she automatically replies, 'Oh, it doesn't matter.'

To be truly urbane, the Egmonter must be quite at home in the sphere to which he has risen. This demands a fair degree of general knowledge, for which this manual is designed to provide a crib.

You must be completely at home in such places as the Sporting Club at Monte Carlo, the Traveller's in Paris, the 21 in New York, the Prado in Madrid, the Palace in St Moritz, Eve in London, the Hotel de la Gavina at S'Agaro, the Plage Sportive at Cannes, the Country Club at Florence, the Cerf in Brussels, Harry's bar in Venice, Formentor in Majorca, the Kildare Street Club in Dublin—all those, just for a start. You must know Ben Russell of the Cunard, George of the Ritz (Paris), Jack Barclay, François André, Charles Winograd, Mario of the Caprice and at least two Editors of national newspapers, half a dozen peers by their first name and a dozen Tory M.P.s.

NAME THROWING

or

NAME DROPPING

DEMANDS

GREAT
FINESSE

George Brown, M.P., is also O.K.

We now come to the Egmonter's art of intelligent name throwing, not like the famous anecdote of the notorious social climber who is reported to have said, 'As I was telling the Queen, I hate name dropping.'

Name throwing or name dropping demands great finesse. First of all, make sure that you have the nickname or first name of a celebrity correct. Here is a guide to nicknames and first names of well-known people which may be thrown at you at a party. If you can memorize them it will help to put you 'in the picture' when names crop up.

Anyone who refers to Sir William Walton as 'Willy Walton' obviously does not know him.

Don't refer to Sir Wavell Wakefield as 'Wakers', he has outgrown it long ago.

It is no good referring to 'my great friend Somerset Maugham'. If he is truly your great friend, you call him Willy.

Eph Smith, the jockey, is pronounced Eeph, because it is short for Ephraim.

It would be as silly to refer to Henry Cotton as Harry as it would be to call Field-Marshal Templer 'Gerry' instead of Gerald.

Rattigan is Terry. Evelyn Laye is Boo. Caesar Romero is Butch. Henry Fonda is Hank. Louella Parsons is Lolly. The Duke of Hamilton is Douglo. Lauren Bacall is Baby. Lord Londonderry is called Whale. Lord Bangor is Eddie. Sir Laurence Olivier is Larry. Vivien Leigh is Viv. Lord Dynevor is Charlie, and his family surname Rhys is pronounced Rice. Hannen Swaffer is Swaff to rhyme with cough. Madame Chanel is Coco. Schiaparelli is Skap. Hugh Beaumont is Binkie. Anatole de Grunwald is Tolly. Richard Dimbleby is Richard. Earl Mountbatten is Dickie. Sir Roderick Brinckman is Naps. The Marquess of Willingdon is Nigs. Antony Asquith is Puffin. Katherine Hepburn is Kate. Sir Alexander Maxwell is Sandy. Sir John Gielgud is John, not Johnny. Sir Dallas Brooks is Dodo or 'the Big Marine'. Peter Finch is Pinch. Christopher Fry used to be called Topher, now he is Kit. Margaret Leighton is Maggie, so is Margaret Lockwood. Florence Desmond is Desi. Prince Frederick of Prussia is Fritz. The Marquess Camden is still Brecky although he succeeded to the family honours long ago. The Duke of Marlborough is Bert. Frances Day used to be called Dolly or Fanny; now it is Frankie. Lady Ravensdale is Irene, pronounced Ireen. Lord Sackville is Titwillow. The Earl of Jersey is Grandy. P. G. Wodehouse and Sir P. F. Warner are both Plum.

The Egmonter must know the 'tops': White's of Orange Street for caviare, Charbonnel et Walker of Bond Street for chocolates, Floris of Jermyn Street for flower-essences and soap, Telfer of Fulham for porkpies, Aylesbury Ltd. for mushrooms, Baxter of the Minories for sausages, Lawrie of Glasgow for bagpipes, Drown of Bond Street for picture restoring, Peter Saunders of

Easton Grey for tweeds, Chivas Regal and Laphroaig as the best single malt whiskies, Frank Smythson of Bond Street for writing paper, Maudie's also of Bond Street for roulette wheels, canasta, backgammon sets and game books, Truslove & Hanson of Sloane Street for calendars and Garrard's for personal clockwinders (only 5 guineas a year).

He must certainly belong to the 400—the dance club in Leicester Square which has become the mecca of distinguished people who want to relax in the knowledge that everything possible is done by the management to keep out snoopers.

He must be able to introduce business friends to functions at several of the Livery Companies in the City—all foreigners being immensely impressed by their architecture, atmosphere, and old-world hospitality.

When talking to Frenchmen, he should always be soppy about La Belle France and never send mimosa to a Frenchwoman: it suggests that her husband is being unfaithful. With Germans, he should talk about Goethe and Leopold von Ranke, who have displaced the generals as father-figures. With the Swedes, he should be extra careful about being punctiliously punctual and always remember to bring flowers—not send them afterwards— whenever invited to a private house for the first time.

He must never refer to Australians as 'Orstrylians'. Someone present may be one and in any case, it is not funny, any more than it is to refer to New Zealanders as Pig Islanders. This also applies to an assumed American accent—Northern or Southern.

With the Irish, he must be fully aware not only of the identity of the six counties outside the twenty-six, but also of The Little Flower. He must never be disparaging about General Franco when with Spaniards.

He must never refer to Buckingham Palace as Buck House or to the War Office as the War House, unless he has been a courtier or in the Brigade. He will never make the mistake of calling the College of Arms the College of Heralds.

As for his figure, he should keep an eye on his waist-line rather than on his weight.

Respect superstitions in other people and never say that you have none yourself. Cultivate the cult.

Remember that peacocks are unlucky (even peacocks' feathers indoors), toy elephants must have their trunks facing the door, a hat must never be placed on a bed, umbrellas must never be opened in a theatre, 'Three Blind Mice' is an unlucky tune among theatrical folk, wild birds presage death if they fly into a private home. But do not overlay yourself with the more ordinary ones, such as walking under a ladder and lighting three cigarettes from a match.

If you have a superstition, let it be a really good one. To say *inshallah* is much smarter than to touch wood.

The profession of swanning or Egmonting is quite new. It is primarily useful to advertising agencies, newspapers and really big business where contacts are all important. If you can learn to swan yourself, while delegating authority to your subordinates, it is a delightful life. It can also prove very fruitful.

Mark you, the accountants must be persuaded to take a long term view of the whole thing and your fellow directors must not be too envious of you.

To be a true Egmonter, you must stay at the best hotels, eat at the best restaurants, play golf on the best golf courses, and, above all, know or get to know the best people. You must be a first-class lady's man, dress well, be a connoisseur of wines and food, in fact, you must be a complete cosmopolitan.

An ability to secure first night tickets, boxes at the opera, ringside seats for big fights, grandstand tickets for Test matches, international rugger matches and cup finals for important clients is a *sine qua non*, irrespective of cost.

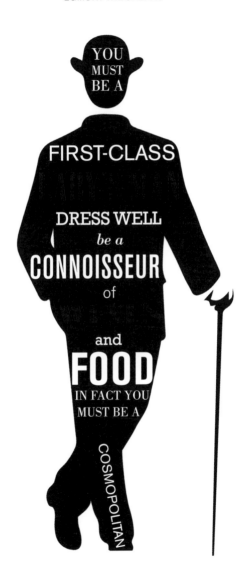

YOU MUST BE A FIRST-CLASS DRESS WELL be a CONNOISSEUR of and FOOD IN FACT YOU MUST BE A COSMOPOLITAN

Your own box at Royal Ascot is a very important matter. Until the alteration to the buildings on the course, it was almost impossible to secure one. You do, of course, secure a far better view from the Royal Enclosure. But there are no facilities for providing hospitality in the form of champagne or a cold luncheon in the Enclosure itself. Anyway, not only you, but also your guests, would have to have passed the scrutiny of Her Majesty's Ascot representative (of which later).

There are still dozens of private boxes at the Albert Hall, inherited from the last century. They, however, are seldom a status symbol in these democratic days of holiday camp get-togethers, dance competitions, political rallies, and mass meetings of various sorts and descriptions.

A private box at Covent Garden is a very different affair, provided that you know enough people who care about opera. Balletomanes are easier to find; you might, therefore, belong to the Sunday Ballet Club.

Never go to the second night of a new play.

Never go to a midnight matinée . . . it's hell.

Add to your general knowledge by looking at quiz programmes on TV, provided that they do not interfere with meal-times.

Never, in fact, allow yourself to become such a martyr to any particular TV programme that it regularly affects the time you take dinner.

Never, we repeat, 'chase' anyone in business.

Avoid garlic and spring onions unless you have some chlorophyll or an Amplex handy.

If you are in the habit of lending books, keep a diary of the people to whom you lend them. Friends are very forgetful.

If you have been offered a drink in a bar or a club, wait for your host to start his before you begin your own.

If you know you are going to a party where there will be a good deal of drinking, swallow a teaspoonful of olive oil beforehand. If you are trapped in a drinking session, it is not bad to order gimlets for yourself. They sound suitably alcoholic, but being a mixture of gin and lime juice, the lime juice largely counteracts the gin.

Never drink a white wine after a red wine—unless it is a glass of Château d'Yquem with your dessert. Follow champagne with brandy, never whisky, even if you have a whisky later on.

If you wake up with a mild hangover, try hock and seltzer. If you have a really bad one, take fernet branca and brandy.

If you are introducing people of the opposite sex, for goodness' sake remember to introduce the man first, unless there is the disparity of, say, introducing an ambassador and a pretty girl. In this case, you say to the ambassador (whom you call Excellency, by the way, except the United States ambassador, who is Mr Ambassador, regardless of sex), 'May I present Miss Reynolds? Miss Reynolds—this is the Bohemia Ambassador' or whatever their names are. He will be delighted.

When shaking hands with a man do not crook the little finger, whatever it may mean. Let the handshake be firm, but not too hard, particularly if it is at a reception. Don't let it be limp, and if you suffer from moist hands, try to do something about it, such as a dab of eau de cologne or talcum powder when nobody is looking. On the whole, handshaking is dying out. Let it die, particularly at a cocktail party when you are introduced to a whole string of people. Don't stick out your hand at all and sundry.

Never kiss a woman's hand even if she is a foreigner or when you are abroad. She will not expect it and you won't do it well. False gallantry is rather silly.

If at a party you meet someone for the first time and your hostess as usual has slurred his name, it is always possible to ask how he spells it. It will be sheer bad luck if it happens to be Jones, which can be spelled only one way.

When Royalty are present, never attempt to leave before they do.

There are far fewer field-marshals than peers, so if you have the occasion to address a peer who is also a field-marshal, address him as a 'Field-Marshal'.

Never mispronounce people's names. If it is Smythe, make sure it is not pronounced Smith—improbable but possible. Never spell their name wrongly. It may be Nichols, Nicholls, Nickols or Nickoles for example. Get it right, even if it means asking their telephone operator.

Avoid boring people with stories about your golf, but listen to theirs.

Never tell people that they look unwell. Tell them the opposite, unless they are real hypochondriacs, and then they don't matter anyway.

If you say 'you make me feel twice the person I am', it is splendidly flattering.

.... DO NOT ....

SUPPOSE

THAT SOMEONE YOU MEET WHO

DRESSES LIKE A

BEATNIK

IS THEREFORE A

LITERARY

~ *or otherwise* ~

ARTISTIC CHARACTER

.... IT IS ....

NOT CLEVER

—— to be ——

DELIBERATELY UNSHAVEN

Do not suppose that someone you meet who dresses like a beatnik is therefore a literary or otherwise artistic character. It is not clever to be deliberately unshaven.

To tell people that they are witty is an infallible way to earn yourself popularity.

Tell a woman that you presume she takes a Double A shoe. It suggests that she has an aristocratically narrow foot.

Internationally it is no longer smart to talk about bull-fighting. Soccer is 'the fried potato'.

If you have a débutante daughter, train her so that she stands arms akimbo, bosom in, chin out. No suggestion of Jayne Mansfield. When you meet an actor or an actress in a theatre dressing-room, you must never criticize them or the play. They are not human while still in their grease painting.

It is now very smart to go ice skating since Princess Anne started to take lessons.

Back to the subject of name-throwing, never refer to Stoneleigh Abbey, Haddon Hall or Blenheim Palace or Warwick Castle in full. It must always be Stoneleigh, Haddon, Blenheim, or Warwick. This applies to all stately homes whether castles like Inveraray Castle or big houses like Luton Hoo.

If you are telephoning a lady of title, such as Lady Robinson, and the call is answered by a servant, you don't say, 'May I speak to her Ladyship?' You say 'May I speak to Lady Robinson?' Only servants use the ladyship phrase. Equally you don't address a peer as 'Your Lordship' unless you are an underling. And for heaven's sake never refer to your own wife as 'the wife' or 'the Mrs' or as 'Mrs Brown' or whatever your name is. Always refer to her as 'my wife' or by her christian name.

With very few exceptions, such as the Guards Club and the Boat Club, never designate a club as such, except to a taxi-cab driver. In other words, it is White's, not White's Club. It is the

Savage, the Athenaeum, the Turf, the Beefsteak. It is scarcely conceivable that anyone would refer to Boodle's as Boodle's Club. And yet it is quite a common mistake for people to speak of the R.A.C. Club, which is tautological, because the R.A.C. stands for the Royal Automobile Club anyway.

Good luggage with no hotel labels on it is another status symbol. Your own shirtmaker and bespoke shoemaker are splendid if you can afford them. All can prove to be useful in making new contacts. There is a camaraderie which can soon lead to better things if the other fellow thinks you have the same and therefore impeccable taste as he has.

Don't wear a button-hole all the year round; it is extrovert, self-conscious, and usually a sign of an inferiority complex deep down.

Never admit illness if you can help it. Play it down as far as possible. Nobody is interested in your symptoms. If you get sciatica, however, you can still call it a slipped disc, though it is not so socially O.K. as it used to be.

Remember that coronary thrombosis is pronounced as spelt, not as cor-own-ary.

If you want to appear in the gossip columns, go to the London Clinic.

It is always smart to go into a hospital or nursing home for a check-up, particularly if there is nothing the matter. It keeps everybody guessing. Your enemies will trust that it is nothing trifling and then you come out and confound them.

Monte Catini is a splendid place for a cure. Vichy is not what it was, socially.

Enton Hall is the place at which to lose weight fashionably. (Dengler's at Baden Baden used to be It.) Enton Hall is also a place where you are likely to make excellent contacts, although you are almost sure to sleep badly.

Baden Baden is ideal, genuinely and socially, for asthma.

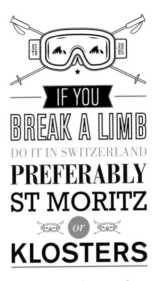

IF YOU
BREAK A LIMB
DO IT IN SWITZERLAND
PREFERABLY
ST MORITZ
or
KLOSTERS

Indeed, to go to any recognized spa in place of the usual casino town (though most spas have casinos anyway) is more or less a status symbol.

If you break a limb, do it in Switzerland, preferably St Moritz or Klosters, but insure yourself before you go and come back by aeroplane, preferably a flying ambulance. It ensures the greatest inconvenience to everyone but yourself, and you stand a fine chance of being photographed at London Airport. Alternatively, do it in the Shires. To break your neck out hunting is the epitome of smartness.

If you truly drink too much and want to stop it, there is a place in Zürich which is unparalleled in its percentage of successful cures, and nobody knows you are there.

If you are still a subordinate and know, for absolutely certain, that you are irreplaceable, a diplomatic illness is a very good thing to have. You can say that your doctor wants you to have a series of X-rays. The inference is that you are going into the private wing of some hospital. It covers a multitude of ills, but does not commit you to any lengthy stay or serious complaint. Equally, you can say that your doctor insists that you go away for a few days or you will crack-up. In this case, the inference is that you are saving your boss from the inconvenience of your having a real nervous breakdown which will put you out of commission for several months.

But you must be damn sure that nobody can really take your place and the boss is left with the feeling that it is largely his fault that you are feeling so poorly, thanks to over-work. By contrast, as a salaried man, you must never allow the illness of your wife or children to interfere with your work unless it is absolutely unavoidable. If it is, state the case as briefly as maybe.

Learn, as soon as possible, the various executive diseases—duodenal ulcers, the symptoms of high blood pressure, migraine, and gout. Gout is a Debrett disease like lumbago, which is often associated with sport, such as hunting. Insomnia is not a bad thing to claim. It suggests that you are working too hard. Diabetes is so prevalent that the diabetic is bound to mention it, if only because of his diet. Nobody minds admitting it nowadays, though it used to be taboo.

It is comforting to know that people with practically any health problem from hardening of the arteries to a coronary can drink whisky, though not gin.

An attack of shingles sounds most unattractive, but it is quite smart, because of its association with nerves.

Your own family physician, as opposed to a National Health doctor, is nowadays a status symbol, quite apart from the fact that he will see you, metaphorically at once, in your own home instead of your queuing up in his surgery.

Never go to a specialist without consulting your own doctor

first. If you do so, and the specialist (known as a consultant) sees you without a chit from your G.P., rest assured that he is a suspicious character.

Remember that a physician is addressed as Dr and that a surgeon is addressed as Mr. Similarly no dentist is addressed as Dr, because he is technically a dental surgeon.

Avoid being operated upon by a surgeon you know personally. An operation should be as cold-blooded as possible—between strangers, so to speak.

Never tip your doctor by increasing his usual fee by a few guineas, however well he has taken care of you or your family. But a case of whisky or champagne will not come amiss.

If you have rheumatism, the smart way to try to get rid of it is to buy one of those copper bracelets, first popularized by members of White's. Do not expect any results for at least two months, wear it continuously and for cleanliness' sake, soap off the discoloration of the skin periodically.

If you have eczema, try Bob Martin's 92. It is as good for humans as it is for dogs.

Apropos of ill health. We always remember Lord Nuffield telling us many years ago that any man of forty who normally enjoys good health is either a fool or his own best doctor. Another tip was bicarbonate of soda for practically anything.

The late Sir St Clair Thomson used to say that in spite of motor-car crashes, wars and aeroplane crashes, the average man can expect to live at least as long as half the combined ages of his mother and father at their respective deaths. He also used to say that men with large lobes to their ears were likely to live to a great age anyway.

If you suffer from cramp—and many people think this is aggravated by over-smoking—try putting half a dozen wine-bottle corks in a muslin bag and then stuff it down between the sheets at the bottom of your bed. Whether this is mere faith-healing or not, it often works.

The old phrase 'an apple a day keeps the doctor away' certainly applies to anyone who knows in his heart of hearts that he is drinking more than he should. True, a certain theatrical lady of title when told that she should eat an apple each time she wanted a drink, replied, 'But darling, I can't eat forty apples a day.' However, that is by the way.

Don't swallow pills just for the hell of it, unless they look so fascinating that they form a topic of conversation. Never be seen sucking indigestion tablets. Incidentally, don't sneer at the idea of sleeping north and south.

If possible, avoid sleeping pills. With very few exceptions, they are the opposite of aphrodisiacs.

There is much to be said for sleeping always on your right side, thus saving any pressure on the heart.

It is curious how many church-going people sleep well. Perhaps it is because they say their prayers just before putting out the light and these act as a buffer between their daytime problems and any risk of consequent insomnia.

One of the most revealing sidelights on a man's character is his choice of books. If you have a chance of looking at your host's book shelves, it will tell you a great deal about him and his wife, if he is married. Collections of bound volumes which are clearly never read show that he is seeking an extra status symbol, being possibly aware that one definition of a gentleman is someone whose grandfather had a library. Not a bad one, incidentally.

If the shelves are full of biographies, it is worth noting a few. They may give a clue to the men he admires and therefore to his own aspirations. If there are travel books on any particular country, that can also be helpful, and provide an extra topic of conversation after dinner.

The Guinness Book of Records is splendid reading and can be immensely useful for settling arguments. Get one at once if you are without it in the home.

Try to acquire a certain amount of off-beat anecdotes on items of polite dinner conversation such as the fact that Haut Brion is a Graves and not a Médoc; that V.S.O.P. stands for very special old pale (brandy); that the last vintage year for Martel was 1913; and that green Chartreuse has the highest alcoholic content of any liqueur.

4

EGMONT

FOLLOWS THE

STRAWBERRIES

TO BE SEEN *in the* RIGHT PLACES at the RIGHT TIME and in the RIGHT CLOTHES is quite an ART

TO BE SEEN in the right places at the right time and in the right clothes is quite an art. So many people are mistaken in thinking that Monte Carlo and Cannes are fashionable in July and August. If the truth be told, many of the rich people who own villas on the Riviera go away to escape the *congés payés* and the rag trade.

No, Monte Carlo and Cannes are very fashionable in January and the first half of February, even though or because they are out of season. This is equally true of St Moritz. Some gossip writers of the national dailies still think that Christmas and the New Year is the High Season there, when, in fact, it starts punctually on 15 February and continues until 15 March, on which date it ends equally abruptly.

The right place for Easter is Le Touquet, just as Deauville is the place in which to see and be seen at Whitsun. Then comes Paris in the spring. London and Ascot is the centre of the world in June, particularly if you are able to wear a Royal Enclosure badge.

Neither Wimbledon nor Henley is truly smart.

In July, you have the option of Goodwood or Race Week at Baden Baden. Any other week than Race Week, when they gamble in gold at the casino, is a total loss. And you *must* stay at Brenner's Hotel.

August gives you the Dublin Horse Show, the Grande Semaine—really a fortnight—at Deauville, and possibly the Lido.

In September, if you are still following the strawberries, you have the choice of Biarritz—but not before the 15th—Cannes and Monte Carlo once again, the last weekend at Le Touquet, Villa d'Este, and, of course, Scotland, which extends into October, when New York becomes fashionable.

November is the only month where no place is really smart. Christmas should be taken at the Mamounia Hotel in Marrakech, unless you go to Estoril.

Most people nowadays go by air, unless they are motoring. Even then, many travellers arrange to be met by hired cars at the airport the other end, which is a reminder that when you read and see photographs of social celebrities going to Nice for their holidays, nothing could be further from the truth. Nice is as bourgeois as Blackpool. It is mentioned merely because it is the nearest airport to Cannes, Monte Carlo, Cap Ferrat, and Antibes—the last being the only really smart place on the Riviera in August, provided that you stay at the Cap Hotel.

Somewhere along the line we seem to have missed out Rome. As long as you do not go there in winter, July or August, it is now very fashionable. The two latest places to visit are Israel and

Beirut. Tel Aviv is becoming almost as smart as New York as a place to know.

Apart from air travel, provided that people will not think you are afraid of flying, there is always the Blue Train, virtually the last of the grand European expresses. Made famous by 'The Madonna of the Sleepings', this dowager duchess of the railway track is something to experience at least once in your life, particularly in the winter. There is still a feeling of romance, of Queen's messengers carrying the bags, of foreign spies and beautiful, unaccompanied maidens as you slide at 60 m.p.h. through la Belle France, pulling up the blinds at eight in the morning to see the mimosa and the deep blue of the Mediterranean only a few yards away.

In every big casino town, there is always at least one recognized meeting place for V.I.P.s. At Cannes, it is Jules' bar. At Monte Carlo, it is Victor's and the Point (in September). At Le Touquet, it is Flavio's. At St Tropez, it is Senequier's. At Deauville, you have the choice of the Normandy, Luigi's and the Royal. At Biarritz, it is the Basque or the Miramar. In Paris, it is the Ritz bar, among many others, and you dine at Maxim's.

The smartest hotel in Venice is the Cipriani. The smartest bar in Rome is the Excelsior.

The smartest high-brow club-restaurant in London is the White Elephant, that is if you want the younger generation of playwrights, actors, actresses. The smartest game to play in a casino is unquestionably *trente-et-quarante*, unless you are a millionaire and play 'Tout Va'. But you are within your rights to stand and watch the big game—*behind* the brass railings—for as long as you like. Don't forget to bring your passport when you enter a casino for the first time. You will look a terrible ignoramus if you fail to do so, or if you try to get your plaques from the man who takes your entrance fee for the Salles Privées. Never play

NEVER PLAY
BOULE
IT IS BOTH
COMMON
and
SILLY

boule. It is both common and silly. If you play roulette, it is smart to tell the croupier to put your money on the finales—say 7, 17, 27 or 2, 12, 22, 32—or on one of the Tirs. A Tir is a series of apparently unconnected numbers. The best way to get a seat at either a roulette or chemin de fer table in a crowded casino is to tip one of the flunkeys and wait for the magic phrase 'La Partie commence'.

The most fashionable way of spending any holiday abroad is undoubtedly to hire a villa. It means that you can eat what you like and when you like, invite people in for drinks which you have bought at the normal wine-shop prices and avoid all fifteen per cent service charges. It also means that, if you are staying in a casino town, you are not automatically canalized into the gaming rooms. Nothing is more sophisticated than to have a rubber of bridge in the South of France. But avoid cut-throat.

Once you have taken a villa holiday, you will probably never want to stay in a hotel again, and if there are four of you it is genuinely cheaper. Besides, what could be smarter than to tell your friends airily that you are taking a villa abroad for your holidays, even if it is on the Costa Brava or in one of the lesser known Italian resorts? And what better way to 'flannel' a prospective client? An invitation to a villa holiday is very hard to refuse, if you couch it properly. This is not an original idea, but so few people do it as yet that it continues to be a remarkably worthwhile ploy.

If you are staying in an hotel and feel that you are sure to need a whisky or a brandy as a nightcap, buy a bottle at the local wine shop and smuggle it up to your bedroom. It is cheaper that way.

Never buy your favourite cigarettes in a hotel in Spain. Buy them from the boot-black, at nearly half the price.

If you want to fool a Spanish boot-black in Madrid or anywhere else, wear suede shoes. There is nothing he can do about it.

Do not forget that the old phrase 'when in Rome do as the Romans' is true of anywhere in the world. Drink the local wines, eat the local food. They will be better and less expensive than anything imported. Notice that local cider in Spain is usually more expensive than a bottle of wine, and that a *trattoria* in Italy is cheaper and often better than a *ristorante* and do not presume that an *osteria* is beneath your notice.

In Switzerland, remember that the food is nearly always better in a regional restaurant than in a big hotel which caters for clients from all over the world and therefore often produces an undistinguished menu.

Remember that, apart from a very small area in the Rhineland, German red wine is not worth drinking, but that the cold venison-pie can be delicious.

Do not be surprised in Portugal if nobody offers you vintage port. It is the wrong climate for this purely English-taste wine. Nor be surprised if taxicabs in Estoril are practically cheaper than tramcars.

In Brussels and other big Belgian cities, it is essential but easy to join a drinking club to enable you to drink spirits, which are officially unobtainable in a restaurant. There are no such troubles in Luxembourg.

If your favourite number at roulette is zero, never gamble in Belgium—there isn't one.

Never wear a white dinner jacket in the South of France. It is embarrassing if someone calls *garçon* at you. But bring a pair of white flannels if you go in September. You can always 'rent a sac'; in other words, hire a set of golf clubs from the local pro.

Always take some Carter's Little Liver Pills and whatever is your favourite antidote to gippy tummy when you go abroad. Rich cooking can spoil the best organized holiday.

The Riviera is now so built-up that mosquitoes are largely a thing of the past at Monte Carlo, Cannes, and the other leading resorts in the South of France. The test is primarily whether there is still a mosquito net over your bed. If there is, use it the first night and then make enquiries as to its necessity.

If you see anyone on the beach with an apparent whiplash on his or her shoulders, beware. It means that Portuguese men-o'-war are around—those horrible jelly fish which can cause excruciating pain and are never mentioned in the brochures.

When abroad, the Egmonter must avoid sticking those transparencies provided by the A.A. and R.A.C. on his windscreen. It suggests that he does not know foreign road signs when he sees them. Nor, of course, should he cover the rear window of his motor-car with those awful sticky labels like 'Napoli'. Apart from being immensely common, they obscure the view.

It is seldom good to Italianize, Germanize or Frenchify famous place names such as Biarritz, Naples (Napoli), Marseilles, Turin (Torino), Munich, Berlin, Capri and St Moritz, but there are

always exceptions such as Lyons, Baden Baden, Juan les Pins. Mentone is better than Menton.

Do not mention the Elgin marbles in Greece.

If you go to Jugoslavia, take a few old suits. They fetch fantastic sums.

Try the Métro in Paris; it is something to have done, like riding a camel in Egypt.

It is highly desirable to have some knowledge of French—if only of the casino variety, such as *banco* and *suivi*. With Le Touquet only eighteen minutes away from Lydd, a complete lack of French is deplorable, despite that delightful maxim, 'English, spoken slowly and with correct articulation is good enough for anybody.'

It is easy enough to buy a 'Brush up your French' or do it by Linguaphone. The traditional way is naturally unsuitable if you are a married man. At any rate, learn enough French to be able to understand a menu in a restaurant.

NEVER ADDRESS
A CONCIERGE
at a
BIG HOTEL
in
YOUR HALTING FRENCH
HE PROBABLY
SPEAKS ENGLISH
JUST AS WELL AS YOU

If the waiter asks you how you like your steak done, remember that if you want it well done you say *bien cuit*; medium is *à point*; rare is *bleu*; very rare is *saignant*.

Never address a concierge at a big hotel in your halting French. He probably speaks English just as well as you. It is different with night porters. Like chambermaids, they seem to be less able to understand English. Head waiters will also be able to understand your English perfectly. But they, like the concierges, are the exceptions to the rule.

Gendarmes are not good linguists. Nor are garage mechanics, but, of course, there are manuals which give you the French for every nut and bolt in your motor-car.

Most caddies in France understand the jargon of golf completely and are usually much more enthusiastic in their search for lost golf balls than those in Great Britain. Very often they are old women.

Always bring back presents of some kind or another from a foreign trip, especially for your domestic staff. Apart from anything else, it saves a great deal of bother at the Customs. Nothing irritates a Customs man more than to be told that you have nothing to declare. After all, it is his job to search and he naturally wants promotion which must presumably depend on his success in detecting smugglers.

Always declare anything dutiable. You cannot afford to make the headlines. On the other hand, it is easy to bore the Customs man and thus get by. Start off with mentioning all the least expensive items—handkerchiefs for your cook, a cheap blouse for your maid, a half-bottle of eau de cologne for your secretary—and so on, naming the price each time. With any luck, he will gloomily mark your luggage with the magic white chalk before you start mentioning the more expensive and dutiable objects. (We hope this book never falls into the hands of the Customs men.)

EGMONT

HOST
AND
GUEST

ENTERTAINING IN THE home ranges from cocktail parties by way of a running-buffet party to a dinner party.

If you decide to do it personally, the best trick is to make it a *champagne d'honneur*, with only soft drinks and one concealed bottle of whisky as the alternative. Reckon on half a bottle of champagne per head and you will be well within the amount required. Put the bottles in a bath tub with an adequate amount of ice to keep them cold. (Your refrigerator will not be big enough.) Produce a few plates of cheese straws and dozens of ash trays. Hope that the guests will not burn your carpets, mantelpieces or tables and that they will leave no later than eight o'clock. One way to achieve this desirable termination is to ask one or two of your closest friends beforehand to say good-bye to your wife in a suitably loud voice round about a quarter to eight. It usually works, though the risk of people staying late is enhanced by the champagne.

HOPE THAT THE GUESTS ···········*will not*··········· BURN YOUR CARPETS MANTELPIECES OR TABLES AND THAT THEY WILL LEAVE NO LATER than EIGHT O'CLOCK

Never ask so many people that there is an uncomfortable crowd. It is done only by hosts and hostesses who are not sure how many of their guests will turn up. When you introduce people to one another, make sure that they can hear each other's names correctly.

If you give a running-buffet party for more than a dozen guests, put all the cold stuff on the centre table. Place the hot dish on a side table. Make sure that there are enough chairs for everybody and that the knives, forks, and spoons are in a prominent position. This may be platitudinous, but it is not always done. Apart from sweets, a large brie makes an admirable sign-off to the meal. Wines should be both white and red, with whisky as well, and there should be any amount of hot coffee.

When they have eaten and drunk their fill, you may persuade the guests to join in 'The Game'—that Hollywood version of charades which though at least twenty years old in this country is always good fun and is not played often enough. If you have invited an actor or actress to the party, they will set the ball rolling.

A running-buffet is primarily to 'work off' your less distinguished friends to whom you feel some kind of obligation. The prime test of successful hospitality is giving a really good dinner party. If you want your wife to be relaxed, get her to hire a freelance Cordon Bleu cook, unless your own is superlatively good. The approximate charge is three guineas, with another guinea or two guineas for an extra parlourmaid or waiter. A hired butler is somewhat ostentatious. Make sure that the parlourmaid is truly a parlourmaid and not a hash slinger. It happened to us once and our face was very red.

The usual practice nowadays is to ask people at eight o'clock for half past eight, to give time for everyone to arrive in good time and to enjoy a dry martini or sherry before dinner. The dry martinis should be really dry and there should be two kinds of sherry, one very dry. Some philistines may prefer a whisky instead and so a decanter must also be available. For fear that some of your guests may arrive late, make sure that your first course will be a buffet dish, such as melon, grapefruit, avocado pear, smoked salmon, prawn cocktail, or *consommé en gelée*, which cannot get cold.

Tell your parlourmaid, or whoever opens the door and announces the guests, the names of all those she does not know, so that she will get them right. When it is time to go into dinner after the announcement, 'Dinner is served, Madam', let your wife lead the way unless there is a particularly distinguished woman guest.

Remember that if there are eight or twelve at the party, you and your wife cannot sit at the opposite ends of a long table. It does not work out mathematically. So you sit at one end with another man at the other.

Do not have tall flowers down the middle of the table. It kills conversation. Let your guests know what wines they are drinking. They will appreciate them more. But do not do it boastfully.

······ *Do not have* ······
TALL FLOWERS
— DOWN THE —
MIDDLE
OF THE TABLE
············ *It* ············
KILLS
CONVERSATION

The hostess must make sure that she eats each course as slowly as the slowest guests to save embarrassment for the latter, rather than hold up the meal for them. When one guest finishes before another, the plate should be left until everyone else has done so.

All drinks are served on the right-hand side of the guest. You yourself take the first sip to make sure that each wine is in good condition. That, incidentally, is when you say 'I hope you'll like this. It is a 1953 Meursault Goutte d'Or', or whatever it may be.

At the end of dinner, when the decanter of port is ready for attention, the hostess must decide whether (a) to make a sign for the women to join her in leaving the room, or whether (b) to stay on for the coffee and brandy. The advantage of (a) is that it gives time for the women to powder their noses first. The disadvantage is that the men are inclined to linger far too long over their port, cigars, and brandy.

Once everyone is out of the dining-room and back in the drawing-room or sitting-room comes the question of whether or not you play cards, even if it is only one table of bridge. Unless there is going to be some momentous announcement on television, never turn on your set. It is an insult to your guests, suggesting that their conversation is so dull that it is not worth listening to. If your wife embarks on a story which you have often heard before, pretend it is new to you, as she will probably do for you.

If you are going to play cards, make sure that they are really clean, that the pencils are sharp and the scorecards are fresh. Above all, announce the house-stakes of so much a hundred. Never put any guest in the predicament of having to play for more than he or she likes.

If you have a roulette wheel and enough different coloured chips and think this would be fun, arrange to have a communal bank. In other words, let everybody put an equal sum into the kitty, so that if it wins, no one is a big loser and equally no one is hurt if it loses. If the original capital is exhausted, it will, of course, be replenished by all and sundry, so that the game can continue. The host usually acts as croupier.

Poker, even for small stakes, can be dangerous and, anyway, women are seldom as good at it as men. As for canasta, that most damnable of games, you must always be prepared for some of your older women guests wanting to play it. Here again, you must announce the house-stakes.

Occasionally, it can be quite amusing to play tiddly-winks for small stakes. Everybody is at heart a 'winker'.

Never suggest chemmy. Someone is almost certain to lose more than enough. Ask Mr John Aspinall.

Arrange that the drinks tray with its whisky and brandy arrives about an hour after you have finished dinner.

Always have ice ready if your guests are American, and do not necessarily bother to have fine wines for them at dinner. Make sure that the dry martini is unbelievably dry. Remember, though, that sole is a great luxury, like grouse and all other game, and that real French champagne will wow all except the more sophisticated. When Americans are sophisticated, they truly are.

Never press vodka on a Russian, brandy on a Frenchman, Burgundy on a Belgian, Chianti on an Italian, port on a Portuguese, or sherry on a Spaniard. Whisky is much more appreciated than anything, even during a meal, however much they may protest politely. True, Burgundy does not come from Belgium, but the Belgians buy just about the best burgundy that money can acquire. (Drink laws are partly responsible for this.) Frenchmen like vintage port, because they cannot get it at home. They also like a really good claret, because most of the best stuff comes to Great Britain and particularly to Scotland. But it must be perfectly *chambré*, which means that unless you have a really good cellar—which is impossible in a centrally heated flat—you get your wine merchant to send it up to you about two days beforehand and then you have it decanted two or three hours before dinner.

If you have German guests to dinner, never offer them a Rhine wine or Moselle. But they will appreciate a really good cognac, not to mention whisky later on. They will also like French red wines, preceded by a Pouilly or something similar.

In other words, practically never offer foreign guests any wines from their own country. They know them, anyway, and theirs are probably better. Some hosts do it to make their guests feel 'at home'. It could not be more wrong.

Similarly, do not offer steaks to Americans, Spanish omelettes or langouste to Spaniards, pasta dishes to Italians, mutton to Australians, lamb to New Zealanders, curry to Indians, duck with slices of orange to Japanese, suckling pig to Portuguese and Luxembourgers, or goulash to Hungarians.

Make sure that your bathroom or bathrooms look really tidy if and when your guests wish to powder their noses, with a suitable array of your own bottles of after-shave lotions, hair lotion, the shaving cream in a good pack and pine essence, and a really good soap. Your wife's contribution needs to include guest hand towels, toilet water, talcum powder, bathsalts—all smelling nice and clean—and possibly a weighing machine.

When entertaining exquisitely, the Egmonter will certainly have Punt e Mes (Carpano) among his bottles of vermouth. He will also offer a dry white port (probably a Sandeman) as an alternative to sherry, say, Garvey's San Patricio, both of which will be suitably chilled, if not iced.

Never put gin or vermouth in a decanter. Put in anything else, whisky, port, any kind of table wine or liqueur. But *never* put gin or vermouth.

The Egmonter will know that the ideal cellar temperature is between 55°–58° F., and if he has no real cellar, he will keep his wines in a cupboard under the staircase in a horizontal position to prevent the corks drying out. He will know too, that the splash of white on an old crusted wine means 'store this side up'. He will decant *all* wines, except champagne, before having them served, particularly mature red wines, which should be stood up for some hours in the dining-room before they are required. White wines should be chilled in the refrigerator for not more than an hour. If he has an ice bucket (which he should), he can place the white wine in it a few minutes after opening.

When decanting a wine, he will know just how to remove the metal cap or wax protecting the cork, before he draws the cork very gently and wipes the lip of the bottle with a napkin before pouring the contents equally gently into the decanter over a light, and stopping the moment that he can see the sediment has reached the shoulder of the bottle and is about to enter the decanter.

When the port is served—clockwise, of course—he will make sure that it never goes back on its tracks, nor that one of his guests is so busily engaged in conversation that he allows it to remain stationary in front of him.

Oddly enough, in Portugal it is quite proper to help your neighbour on your right before helping yourself.

As he (the Egmonter) will only serve good brandy, he would never dream of having his balloon glasses warmed, except by the hands of his guests as they cup them before tasting. He will be amused if any of the aforesaid guests (unless they are wine shippers) hold their wineglasses by the pedestal, but will be sad if they hold their champagne round the glass itself—if, that is, he serves champagne. In which case, it will come after the red wine.

The ignorant sneer at the 'ritual' of wine drinking. It merely means that they are jealous of their inability fully to enjoy what 'maketh glad the heart of man'.

And that, in a single phrase, is exactly the job of a good Egmonter.

The art of being a good host at a business luncheon or dinner is much more tricky than many people realize. First of all, you must take your guests to some place where you are well-known and where you can secure a table against the wall and not in the centre of the room. If oysters are in season, set the ball rolling by saying that you personally will have some. The inference is that the sky is the limit and guests who might otherwise have been too coy to order them can do so without embarrassment. On the other hand, it is overdoing it to ask for caviare or to order champagne for luncheon. By the way, cold Vichyssoise soup is smart and inexpensive like avocado pears and gulls' eggs.

THE
IGNORANT
SNEER
AT THE RITUAL
OF WINE DRINKING.
IT MERELY MEANS
THAT THEY ARE
JEALOUS
OF THEIR INABILITY
FULLY TO ENJOY WHAT
MAKETH
GLAD THE
HEART OF MAN

Obviously, different people have different tastes, but to ask for slightly unusual dishes shows that you are a man of the world. *Escargots* or *moules marinières* are cases in point. When it comes to an egg dish, *oeufs florentines* are a good choice like sole *mornay* for the fish course. A steak *diane* with its attendant chafing dish is both light and elegant. Stilton or a really good brie are the right choice after the sweets, such as zabaglione, if you can eat any more.

Wines? This is indeed a problem, depending, of course, on what you are going to have. A white burgundy will go with both fish and meat, like a rosé.

If you do not know the word *sommelier*, ask in a restaurant for the wine waiter, not the wine butler. And remember that the restaurant manager is not the head waiter, who is a much inferior person.

But unless you have ordered in advance, you must give your guests the chance to choose. And if any one of them is supposed to have any real knowledge of wines, hand him the wine list and flatter him by asking him to make the selections himself.

Always offer port, and if more than two of your guests accept, order a half-bottle or even a bottle and have it decanted at the table. Always remember to take the first sip yourself—unless you have left it to one of your guests to make the choice; in which case, he will do it. After the coffee, never forget to offer liqueurs and cigars. It is surprising how many self-made men prefer cigars to wines and it makes all the difference to the meal for them.

To be able to talk with modest knowledge about cigars is a great business asset. It shows you are a man of the world. Green cigars, for example, indicate cigars which are still newly-rolled. The best way to cut a cigar is quite simply to use a cigar cutter. If you push a match down the end, it produces a tight little wad. There is no harm in light coloured spots on the outer wrapper.

Once upon a time, connoisseurs actually preferred them. A cigar at the end of a row is no better than the ones in the middle. Pinching a cigar and listening to the crackle does not mean a thing, except to someone in the trade.

There are five terms to denote the shades of Havana cigars:

Claro	light
Colclaro	medium
Colorado	dark
Colorado-maduro	very dark
Maduro	almost black

Many good friendships have been made and lost over a good cigar. There is a curious sympathy between cigar smokers as there is between owners of dachshunds. It is a kind of freemasonry in big business. But your host will be secretly hurt if you puff fiercely as soon as you have lighted up. He would much prefer to see you turn the cigar in your mouth so that it starts with an even glow after you have drawn very gently.

Always be unhurried and careful in the removal of the ash. Flick it off gently with your little finger, leaving a little of the ash to prevent the end growing too hot.

Think of any of your business acquaintances who regularly smoke good cigars and it is odds on their being successful in business. Cigar smokers know that, at the end of a business luncheon, the lighting and smoking of a cigar gives them just those pauses for thought which a keen deal may need. A cigar to a business-man is much the same as a fan to the Victorian débutante. It can be used as a kind of defensive armour. It can be used almost provocatively. In any event, it adds consciously to the smoker's importance in the eyes of the rest of the world.

Never light one cigarette from another. Never talk with a cigarette in your mouth. Never let it droop from your lips. Never put a used match back into a box, however tidy it may appear. Never leave a cigarette burning anywhere—in an ashtray or on a mantelpiece. Don't go on continuously handing round cigarettes to your guests. Never smoke between courses.

To return to eating-out—never, of course, by yourself—this is a social exercise which deserves deep study. The tests of a good restaurant fall into a number of categories. How well do they cook guinea fowl? Ditto, turbot? How good is their hors d'oeuvre? Can they do a steak *diane*?

Be very careful in the choice of the hotel or restaurant to which you take a business guest. If he is important, the Savoy, the Dorchester, the Connaught, the Berkeley and Claridges will not only be well-known to him but may also appear a trifle pretentious, while the Hyde Park Hotel may be too far away from his office.

It is a wise plan to use some really good but slightly off-beat restaurant, where, incidentally, there are not likely to be any eavesdroppers or other businessmen who may be inquisitive about your *tête-à-tête*. (Places like the Aperitif Grill, the Ivy or the White Tower make a pleasant change for the usual business man.)

During the war when he was Prime Minister and wished to have a luncheon party where nobody was likely to see him or his guests arriving and departing, Sir Winston Churchill frequently patronized the Great Western Hotel at Paddington Station—in a private room, of course.

But whatever the restaurant, remember that there is a great art in making waiters your friends and influencing chefs. Never clap your hands, snap your fingers or say 'Psst' to catch a waiter's eye. Say *Dis* (pronounced 'Dee') or *garçon*.

Has it ever occurred to you when you enter a restaurant to wonder what the restaurant manager and the waiters are thinking of you? What quick assessment they make if it is your first visit? What memories they have of previous occasions? Behind the polite, deferential exterior, will lurk many emotions which can affect the success of your luncheon or dinner party one way or the other.

If a top-class restaurant manager does not want your custom, you will be placed near a serving table with all the attendant clatter of waiters coming in and out of the kitchen and you will have to wait an inordinate time before each course.

Making yourself popular in a restaurant is not just a question of flamboyant tipping. Indeed, some managements are grateful if you do not tip at all in the event of your receiving unintentionally bad service.

When you call for the bill and do not propose to pay cash, don't say 'Bring me a cheque form'. Just ask if you can pay by cheque, and when you sign it, do not make it indecipherable. Above all, do not be in a hurry if you want a really good meal.

If, by any chance, a hot dish arrives tepid, or the plates are cold, or a wine tastes wrong, you should certainly send back the dish and if you really know about wine you should smell the cork, send back the bottle and ask for another.

If you are not an expert, you should ask the *sommelier* to taste it. If you are still doubtful, ask for the *maître d'hôtel* to give you his opinion. Never show off in front of your guests by making unjustifiable complaints.

A difficult customer is always a challenge to a good restaurant. But if you are deliberately awkward, you will find, when you next telephone for a table, that they are all engaged.

The square mile of London's West End is a village compared with the hundreds of restaurants in Paris in which you can get lost. In London, every restaurant manager of importance knows all the others and the grape-vine is in continuous operation. You are never asked to take your custom elsewhere and, indeed, if you make a written complaint, you will receive a most tactful reply from the secretary of the company, but you will be put on the black list. Yet, what is truly surprising is the extraordinary self-control of the staff when clients make idiots of themselves. Never a smile passes their lips. Never a scowl furrows their forehead. The *maître d'hôtel*, if called upon, is full of apologies and offers to rectify anything and everything. But that is the end of them and their parties in that particular restaurant.

If you have invited someone to a business luncheon, do not do the silly conventional thing of keeping tactfully off the subject on hand until you have reached the coffee stage. By then, there is no real time to get down to business and you have wasted your money. You should not, of course, start talking shop the moment the other fellow arrives. Give him a chance to swallow his cocktail and order his food before broaching the subject.

On the whole, business luncheons are often a waste of time if you are trying to set up a deal. They only make real sense when you are consolidating a situation already under control.

If, instead, somebody invites you to lunch to talk business, he is obviously going to try to sell you something. So all the above advice works in reverse. Hold off the subject until the last minute when he starts to get desperate.

If you are dining out in a private house, always remember that you must address the woman on your left at least as often as the one on your right, however dull one may be and however fascinating the other.

If your host and hostess are laying on the meal without maids, offer to help when the first lot of plates are to be cleared. If your hostess says 'no', remember you are probably more trouble than you are worth and, having made the gesture, sit still and do nothing. There will probably be one man friend or woman friend already primed to do the job.

Make sure, when accepting the invitation, what clothes you are to wear and if you are invited at eight for half past arrive at about a quarter past eight, not too early and not too late. Always accept or refuse formal invitations in the third person.

Don't be surprised in France if your hostess is sometimes helped first. It is done on the same principle of the host tasting the wine first, to make sure that it is all right.

Do not punish your host's brandy or whisky unduly.

Never, of course, get tight, which may happen unintentionally

Never — *of course* — **GET TIGHT** WHICH MAY HAPPEN **UNINTENTIONALLY** IF YOU HAVE BEEN TO A **PREVIOUS** COCKTAIL PARTY — and — THE ROOM IS **VERY WARM**

if you have been to a previous cocktail party and the room is very warm.

Never use a fish knife if you can possibly avoid it. Make do with a fork.

Do not sit with crossed knees at table. Never let your bare flesh show above your socks if you are fully dressed.

Without necessarily wanting to be the life and the soul of the party, you can always make yourself a more interesting character if you have certain out-of-office accomplishments. You must be able to dance well enough not to tread on your partner's toe; but don't be an extrovert, using up more floor space than is necessary.

Some knowledge of graphology is also useful. You can always acquire an audience at a party by saying that you can read handwriting. If you truly can do so, it is a most valuable accomplishment. La Bohémienne, the resident soothsayer at the Sporting Club and Hotel de Paris, Monte Carlo, is paid large fees by American business-men to elucidate the character of applicants for jobs, promising executives and fellow directors. Handwriting is most revealing about character—meanness, generosity, ostentation, lack of drive, inattentiveness to detail, inferiority complex, and the like. Any cheap manual will teach the fundamentals.

A knowledge of palmistry is only for amusing young people, but it has its uses. Talk about astrology, know your own sign of the Zodiac, but never pretend that you can cast horoscopes. It is too difficult and takes far too long.

If you can't play a musical instrument, at least own a tape-recorder and a hi-fi, the more stereoscopic the better.

Do not monopolize the richest man or the prettiest girl in the party. Make much of the ugliest woman. Her husband is probably very well off, or he would not have married her.

Keep some track of sales at Sotheby's and Christie's, so that you can talk tolerably well on the subject. It is a far better gambit of conversation than the theatre or even the movies.

Never discuss business, even if you suspect that you have been invited for that very purpose, if you can possibly help it. It will suggest that you are in no hurry.

Try to keep off the subject of politics. In spite of an affluent society, tempers can run high. Also remember that pacifists are very belligerent.

If you are telling Stock Exchange stories after dinner when the women have gone out, for goodness sake keep them short and, if possible, avoid the four letter words.

If you play bridge, do not over-call or try to play every hand. On the contrary, you make yourself very popular in becoming dummy often. Never be unkind to your partner. The best players are always the best-mannered. The reverse, too, is usually true. Never lay down your hand unless you are 101 per cent sure that it is unbeatable without finessing. Lose well and win better. Neither is easy. But there is no harm in suggesting that you cut for seats if you are having a losing run.

If you go 'gin' at gin rummy, don't announce it boastfully or in a blasé way.

If your opponents draw all four red threes at Canasta, do not complain about the shuffling or congratulate them on their skill at cards.

If your hosts have dogs, never offer them a titbit at table or afterwards. Nor invite them to join you on a sofa. They have probably been trained never to do so.

Never fiddle with your host's television or radio set unless he expressly asks you to do so. It is an infuriating habit.

Always bring a cheque form in case you find that you are going to play cards.

Do not be the last to leave.

At all costs send flowers next day with a brief thank-you note. The older the hostess, the more she will like being 'bunched'.

If you are in a country house party, never laugh at breakfast. Preferably say nothing except for a muttered 'good morning' and then immerse yourself in a newspaper. Do not, at all costs, follow Field-Marshal Montgomery's wartime injunction to 'Jump out of bed with a glad shout'. Ugh.

If it is your first visit to a particular country house, find out discreetly from a fellow guest what he plans to tip the butler and/ or members of the staff. If you are not enjoying the party, you can always send yourself a telegram, but never from the nearest post office.

As for yachting and sailing, if he is asked for a day, a weekend or more, the Egmonter will make sure exactly what he needs and the kind of craft he will be in. To be quite certain of this, he will ask his host what he should wear. This will clearly depend on the size of the craft—anything from a five-tonner to something very important. He knows that he will be as uncomfortable on a yacht in jeans and a polo-neck sweater as he would be in a 'Dragon' in white flannels blue blazer and yachting cap. (A friend of ours did just that in 1940 and found, when he went aboard, that he was on his way to Dunkirk.)

If his host warns him that they will probably be taking tea on the Squadron Lawn, he will bring a dark blue serge suit. If he belongs to no yacht club, he will, if he has time, arrange for plain black buttons with an anchor on them to be sewn on to it. (Gieves will do the necessary.) He will know that a yachting cap is incongruous for anyone who is not used to yachts. A soft, floppy brimmed, blue or white round canvas hat must be preferable. If there is any question of dining ashore, he will know that he needs to bring a dinner jacket with him, but that, on the whole, it is better not to overdo things.

In no circumstances should he wear 'co-respondent's shoes'.

**IN
NO CIRCUMSTANCES
SHOULD HE WEAR
CO-RESPONDENT'S
SHOES**

6

EGMONT

SPEAKS

HAVING MADE YOUR contacts, you must make sure not to upset them by ignorance of the Queen's English as spoken by the well-to-do. Professor Alan Ross wrote an essay on sociological linguistics which received wide notice in the Press some years ago, because of his introduction of U and Non-U. Much of it is embarrassing, or self-evident. It is already a social fact that anyone who refers to U and Non-U is automatically Non-U.

Fifty years ago, the phrase M.I.F. was coined by the late Lady Pembroke. It referred to people who put their Milk In First when taking tea. This still holds good as a social criterion though doubtless it tastes better that way. You damn yourself with equal certainly if you talk about a quid instead of a pound, pound-note, or sovereign, though the last-named is becoming a trifle archaic like the habit of calling 'Cab' or 'Keb' instead of 'Taxi' when you want a taxi-cab. Cab or keb goes back to the days of the hansom-cab, and the driver knows at once that you are a regular cab user and will therefore stop for you, because he knows that you will not be mean about tipping him. Try it sometime. It works wonders.

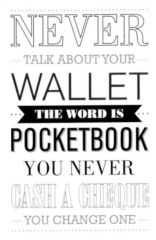

NEVER
— TALK ABOUT YOUR —
WALLET
··· THE WORD IS ◄···
POCKETBOOK
YOU NEVER
CASH A CHEQUE
— YOU CHANGE ONE —

Never talk about your wallet. The word is pocketbook. You never cash a cheque; you change one. You never purchase anything; you buy it. You help; you never assist. You wash; never perform ablutions.

A mansion is technically a house with two staircases, but you only mention the word if you are an estate agent; otherwise you refer to a house.

Never shorten the words telephone or photograph.

Never refer to 'Town' when you mean London. Like Oxford and Cambridge to which you go up, you go up to London, even if you are in Manchester.

Never use the word 'fat' except in its literal sense. Don't speak of 'fat jobs' or 'a fat lot of good that will do you'.

Never say 'I couldn't care less'. It's rude, common, and usually untrue.

In spite of Emily Post, the great American expert on etiquette, there is nothing the matter with referring to other men as fellows or chaps.

A vase is pronounced 'varze', not 'vayze'.

CANNES IS PRONOUNCED WITHOUT THE FINAL 'S' **BUT THE 'T' OF** MOËT ET CHANDON IS PRONOUNCED *and* **KRUG IS PRONOUNCED KROOG**

Cannes is pronounced without the final 's', but the 't' of Moët et Chandon *is* pronounced, and Krug is pronounced Kroog. Never call a top hat a topper, it is vulgar in the extreme. If it is black—and therefore mostly worn at a funeral—it is a silk hat. Otherwise it is a white top hat, or tall hat, as used at Ascot and weddings. *Con*troversy is pronounced with the accent on the first syllable, not con*trov*ersy.

It is very common to use the word 'wealthy'. Rich, well-to-do, very well off are all right.

Never pronounce golf as though it rhymed with the first syllable of doleful. A bicycle is never a cycle or bike, any more than Monte Carlo is Monte.

Never, when giving or answering a toast, say 'Cheerioh', 'Down the hatch' or 'Here's how'. Make a non-committal noise and smile. 'Cheers' is just permissible.

A tail coat is a tail coat and not a dress suit, whatever off-the-peg tailors may call it. Ditto, a dinner jacket is not a dinner suit. And if your hostess tells you to come in a white tie, she means full evening dress and your wife wears white gloves.

Remember that whis*key* is Irish, but whis*ky* is Scotch. Bourbon is pronounced Burbon and if you want a dry martini in France you ask for a *dri*.

Never say 'drunk as a lord'. It has no meaning today.

There is no such thing as a serviette in polite society. It is a napkin—and never tuck it under your chin, even when eating asparagus.

Don't say handbag. Say 'bag', just as lavatory paper is lavatory paper and not toilet paper. Expunge the word 'toilet' from your vocabulary, except for toilet water.

Never refer to *the* Albany. It is Albany, and it has no flats. It has setts or chambers.

Don't call television 'the telly'. It is such an obvious form of inverted snobbism.

Never make puns, unless they are terribly good.

In football, people kick goals. They no more hit them—except in badly-written sports pages—than they kick runs at cricket. It is an East End vulgarity derived from hitting someone a kick.

Never pronounce the first 'e' in pomegranate. Never have cosy little chats, though there is no reason why you should not call someone 'cosy'.

A girl of good family refers to her mother as mummy, not mother, and to her father as daddy, not father.

Never call a soft hat a 'trilby', unless you are a detective—which you are not.

When somebody mispronounces a word, try not to use it yourself in the same conversation.

Never say 'I told you so'.

Avoid 'one for the road', 'have the other half', 'have another'.

Scones are pronounced 'skons'.

Never refer to a lounge unless it is in a hotel, or a couch or settee. Don't call your motor-car 'a nice little bus'. Refer to a magazine as such, not as a 'book'. Never refer to the newspaper you don't take as a 'rag'.

Never call an eye glass a monocle and never wear one unless one eye is genuinely very much better than the other.

Never say 'she did'; give the woman her name. Never say 'pardon'; say 'excuse me'. Don't say 'Like I told you'; it is 'As I told you'. Never 'pass a remark'. Never be 'pleased to meet' someone.

It is 'in the circumstances', not 'under the circumstances'.

Always refer to W.1, not to West 1.

The 'mink and diamond set' is as common as the gossip writers who use the phrase. Anyway, sable is much more expensive than mink.

Do not use dated catch phrases, such as 'out of this world' or 'fabulous'. They are as olde worlde as 'ripping' or 'top-hole'. Never say 'Jolly good show' or 'smashing'.

NEVER CALL A SOFT HAT A TRILBY UNLESS YOU ARE A DETECTIVE, WHICH YOU ARE NOT.

There is no such thing as a cravat. It is a stock—if you have to use the word.

Never follow certain gossip writers and use phrases such as plushy, lush, posh, or snooty. (Posh, incidentally, is a travel clerk's abbreviation for 'Port Out Starboard Home', indicating that the traveller going to the East wants to be on the shady side of the ship both ways.)

If, by any chance, you are ever knighted and become, say, Sir Harry, try to stop dragging your title into the conversation more than four times every half hour. Do not, in a speech, keep on using phrases such as 'the moment he recognized me he said "Well, Sir Harry . . ."' or 'then she contradicted me. "Sir Harry," she joked, "really, I can't believe that, Sir Harry".' Know what we mean?

If making a speech, don't play with your spectacles, putting them on and off as you talk (that is, if you wear spectacles). It can be quite maddening for your listeners.

Never refer to horse-back riding and remember that you 'kill' a salmon.

Never, in conversation, refer to your domestic staff as domestics or servants. If they are women, they are 'maids' and a butler is not a butler if he does not have at least one footman under him. He is your 'man'. Bachelors need to be careful about having only a valet to look after them. It is inclined to look slightly suspicious nowadays if they are young.

If anyone greets you with 'How do you do?', the reply is 'How d'you do?' and not 'I'm very well, thank you' or words to that effect. Never say 'I thought to do' or 'It looks to be'; you must say 'I thought of doing', or 'It looks as if'.

A valet is pronounced as spelled and not as 'valley'.

A cigarette is never a smoke or a fag; never ask for a 'double' port or 'double' martini, ask for a large one. Never say 'Between you and I'; it is ungrammatical and egotistical. The right phrase is 'Between you and me'. Never refer to 'bubbly' or 'champers'; if you mean champagne call it champagne, unless it happens to be Veuve Clicquot, in which case you can call it 'the Widow'. 'Commence' is a bad word. Use 'start' or 'begin'. Never call a bearskin a busby. Remember that dinner is an evening meal. If you want someone to pass the pepper or salt, ask for it by name. Never mention the cruet.

If you are ever presented to the Queen or other women members of the Royal Family, remember that Ma'am is pronounced 'Marm'.

Never say 'Right you are', 'here's How', 'happy days', 'chin-chin', 'What's yours?'.

'Cheery' is a common word, almost as bad as condiments.

It is 'Trooping the Colour', not 'the Trooping of the Colour'.

Never refer to well-known people merely by their christian names unless you are genuinely on christian name terms with them. It is so easy to be caught out.

Avoid the word 'literally', unless you really mean it.

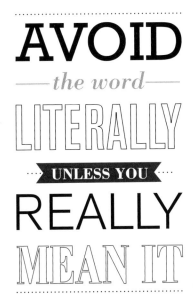

AVOID
—*the word*—
LITERALLY
···◆ **UNLESS YOU** ◆···
REALLY
MEAN IT

If a Lieutenant-Colonel becomes a full Colonel, you can say that he has 'taken flannel'.

Quoting from *Alice in Wonderland*, *Alice Through the Looking Glass* or *Peter Rabbit* is always an elegant thing to be able to do.

If you want to go to the lavatory, go to the loo. Women go and powder their noses.

Never say 'Well, *act*ually' in conversation.

If anyone uses the phrase (*a*) and (*b*) in conversation, he is probably a newspaperman.

In smart theatrical circles, schoolboy slang is coming back like 'goody goody gumdrops', 'super' and 'jolly good'.

Never use the words 'berk' or 'bull'. Both have revolting connotations. Fortunately, the American army's Snafu has been forgotten, witty though it was.

Hubris is a much better word than arrogance. It suggests, for one thing, that you know some Greek.

Remember that the accusative of who is whom. To ask, like the gossip writers, 'who kissed who?' or 'who told who?' is as bad as saying 'between you and I'.

Never split an infinitive.

Amateur is pronounced as spelled, not 'amacheur'.

Always refer to a knave, never to a jack in a pack of cards.

White is pronounced as spelled with an 'H' in it.

Medicine is never pronounced as a trisyllabic. It is 'medsin'.

Margarine is pronounced MarJarine, whatever the makers say.

Formidable is not pronounced 'formiddable'. Exquisite has the accent on the first syllable, not as if it were spelled 'exquizzite'. Croquet is pronounced 'croaky', not 'croakay'.

Venison is pronounced 'venzon'.

By the way, you pronounce ungallant and gallant (except in the sense of courageous) with the accent on the last syllable.

Edwardian is pronounced Edwawdian, and because is pronounced becoz.

Always avoid the word 'chic', even if you pronounce it correctly as 'sheek'.

Madame Tussaud is pronounced Tooso.

'Frisco is a vulgarism. It is San Francisco.

You do not pronounce the 'l' in golf.

St Tropez is pronounced as spelled, but preferably St Trop.

Ascot is pronounced as Ascut, with the emphasis on the first syllable.

Ibiza is pronounced Ibbeetha. Klosters is pronounced with a long o.

Never pronounce Capri as Capree.

If you are in any doubt about the pronunciation of foreign words, such as lingerie, soigné, fiancée, do not use them in

England. But remember that your English accent is as attractive to a French girl as her French accent when talking English is attractive to you. We don't know why, but this is so.

.... **BUT** ....

REMEMBER

.... THAT YOUR ....

ENGLISH ACCENT
is as

ATTRACTIVE

———— *to a* ————

FRENCH GIRL
as her

FRENCH ACCENT
.... *when* ....

TALKING ENGLISH
IS ATTRACTIVE
TO YOU

7

EGMONT

IN THE

OFFICE

A FIRST-CLASS, well educated secretary is at least as essential to a successful man as an intelligent wife.

An intelligent, efficient secretary, who is also personable and of a pleasant disposition, is very difficult to find. When you have found her, cherish her.

Don't forget she is a human being with a home to go to and friends to meet outside her official office hours. There are bound to be days when you will unexpectedly keep her on overtime. If you make her late for a personal engagement, tell her to pay for a taxi out of the petty cash. This reaps dividends. On future occasions, she will stay with a smile and you will get the reputation of being a generous and thoughtful employer.

Don't treat her like a moron. If she is one, why are you employing her? Her spelling and grammar, at least, are probably better than yours.

DON'T TREAT HER **LIKE A MORON** IF SHE IS ONE **WHY ARE YOU** EMPLOYING HER? HER SPELLING *and* GRAMMAR AT LEAST **ARE PROBABLY** BETTER THAN YOURS

Let her make personal telephone calls in the office. If she is a secretary worthy of you, she won't overdo it. It is unlikely that, along with her other qualifications, she is clairvoyante, so tell her where you are going when you leave the office for any length of time, and also keep her in the picture where work is concerned.

In return for a little consideration and a good salary, she will tell lies for you, do her best to achieve the impossible, bear with your tantrums and eccentricities, humour you, nurse you, even sew on your buttons, buy your Christmas presents and do a hundred and one chores, in addition to her normal secretarial duties, to make your time in the office more comfortable. Treat her badly and she can make your life a complete hell, while still doing her work efficiently.

Don't forget that a good secretary may well have friends and relatives who are P.A.s to chairmen, directors, M.P.s, and people of position and influence. If she thinks well of you, she will tell them so . . . and the reverse.

But how to find this treasure? Far the best way is to contact one of the top secretarial bureaux. They will make a note of your requirements and send only those applicants they consider suitable. Advertising in *The Times* and *Daily Telegraph* presents a hazard. Unless your advertisement is attractive and unusual, you may receive no replies at all. On the other hand, an outstanding advertiser will be inundated with applicants. Provided you have plenty of time to spare, these can be amusing; but half will prove completely unsuitable and a good number will be from chronic advertisement-answerers, who have no intention of taking the job anyhow.

Don't be displeased if visitors to your office stop to talk to your secretary. She is probably not revealing some closely guarded trade secret, but is just being pleasant. If they start inviting her out to lunch, however, there may well be cause for alarm, as they may be proposing to marry the girl, or lure her away from you with offers of a larger salary.

It is an excellent thing to be complimented on your secretary's efficiency and charm of personality. It shows your astuteness and knowledge of human nature in selecting her in the first place, and the superiority and force of your character that such a paragon continues to work for you when, obviously, there must be great competition for her services. Glowing comments on her physical attributes are not so flattering to her employer, for these may be of an ambiguous nature.

Private secretaries should be seasoned, not battleaxes, of course; but preferably in their thirties or later.

If they make all your travel arrangements for you, be sure that they use a really good travel agency, whether or not they get a few 'perks' as a result.

If your secretary puts flowers in your office, do not assume that she is in love with you—she may just like flowers.

············· IF YOUR ·············

SECRETARY

────── *puts* ──────

FLOWERS

IN YOUR OFFICE

DO NOT ASSUME THAT

────── she is ──────

IN LOVE WITH YOU

SHE MAY JUST

LIKE FLOWERS

Beware of employing a débutante. Your friends may be impressed to hear your secretary is the Lady Lucy Lockett; she may be charming and a painstaking if rather slow stenographer and most obliging in taking her holidays in the winter because she enjoys winter sports. But, unhappily, when the summer comes, you may find that absences to attend Royal Garden Parties, Ascot, Goodwood and so forth are considered as essential as a visit to the dentist is to the less socially elevated girl.

Secretaries with independent means should also be regarded with suspicion. Though often prepared to accept a lower salary, they are also liable to leave at a minute's notice if you displease them.

If you employ a chauffeur, make sure he is a teetotaller, if possible.

The art of writing private letters is rapidly going out with the almost universal use of the telephone. Many people have forgotten how to write in the third person when they are addressing someone of great importance to whom they are writing for the first time. This, of course, is the most formal way of starting a letter, followed by 'Dear Sir', 'My dear Mr Robinson', 'Dear Mr Robinson', 'Dear John Robinson', 'Dear Robinson', 'Dear John'. The sign-off in order of growing familiarity is 'Yours faithfully', 'Yours truly', 'Yours sincerely', 'Yours very sincerely', 'Yours ever' or 'Ever yours', and 'Yours affectionately' to a woman. 'As ever' is a crafty sign-off. It can so easily mean 'As never'. 'Yours cordially' or 'Cordially yours' is American.

The nuances in French are so delicate that you must really find a Frenchman to decipher them for you. For example, we still do not quite know where '*Je vous serre la main*' comes in.

When writing a business letter, it is always a good plan to keep it on one side of the writing paper, and if it is typewritten, it is much politer to write the 'Dear Mr Robinson' in your own hand, likewise the 'Yours sincerely' at the other end.

AS EVER
is a
CRAFTY SIGN-OFF
IT CAN SO EASILY MEAN
AS NEVER

It is also a good plan to introduce at least one unusual word in the letter. If, for example, you are genuinely baffled by something and use the word 'hornswoggled', it is sure to create an impression.

If you want an interview, it is advisable to end by saying 'I will telephone your secretary to find when it would be convenient to come and discuss the matter'. If you merely say 'When can we meet?' your inquiry may go unanswered. Too many business letters answer themselves.

If you are really angry about something when dealing with someone of importance to you, write the letter as furiously as you like. But then don't post it—just keep it in a drawer. A few days later, if you reread it, you will realize what a fool you would have been to send it.

If you are abroad, it is not a bad idea to send amiable and preferably witty coloured post cards to business associates of the most expensive place on your tour, but make sure that each is differently worded in case the recipients meet during your absence.

Never write or sign any business letter with anything but a real pen. The various writing instruments, to use a generic phrase, are excellent in their own way for inter-office memos and correcting proofs. But they deprive the handwriting of character and this is especially dangerous in applying for a big job or important interview.

Don't dictate through a pipe, with your head out of the window, practising golf shots, or half underneath the desk when stooping for something. If you must do these things in order to concentrate, be tolerant of the results.

A little perambulation is permissible, but do try to stay in the same room.

Never space a letter in such a way that when the recipient turns over leaf he merely finds your signature on the other side. It is infuriating.

If anyone writes to congratulate you on any promotion or advancement, send your reply in your own handwriting. Never have it typed.

If you ever have the time, it is no bad thing to copy the late George Bernard Shaw and learn shorthand. It can be a godsend, provided that you can read it back.

Those electric typewriters which make it look as if the words have been printed instead of typed are a real status symbol—most impressive.

Quite as important as writing a good business letter, always on good writing paper and preferably with your name engraved on the top of it, is the interpretation of business letters which you receive yourself.

The Naval glossary is a very good guide to the deciphering of hidden meanings. Thus:

With reference to: Whether it has or not, this letter must start somehow.

Considering the wider aspects of the case: I have very narrow views on the subject myself.

I approach the subject with an open mind: Completely ignorant of the whole affair.

Under consideration: Not under consideration.

Under active consideration: Propose instituting a search for the file.

Concur generally: Haven't read the paper and don't want to be bound by anything I say.

Snowed under: Only able to take an hour and a half for luncheon.

This will be borne in mind: No further action will be taken until you remind me.

Being dealt with separately: Perhaps, but with any luck will be forgotten entirely.

You will remember: You have forgotten, if indeed you ever knew.

All orders issued by my predecessor are to remain in force: I haven't read them yet, but shall take the first opportunity of altering them when I do.

In due course: Never.

As you know: As you don't know.

You will appreciate: You are far too dense to understand this.

Similarly, in the business world:

We are afraid we have no job at the moment at the money you obviously command: We haven't the slightest intention of offering you one at the very modest sum we know you would accept.

We have considered your proposition most carefully, but regret that we have come to the conclusion that at the present moment we are not in a position to employ your services: It was always quite out of the question, but it gives us an excuse for not answering your letter sooner.

Keep in touch: Don't keep in touch.

We hope that our association will be a long and happy one: We propose to give you a brief try-out and will fire you the minute you fail to achieve the impossible.

We regret that at the present minute there are no vacancies, but: We don't owe you a living, you dope.

If you have any other ideas, please keep us in mind: For goodness sake, keep out of our hair.

We will be writing to you shortly: Forget it.

If at any time we can be of service to you: We are not sure that you can pay now, but there is always a chance that you might in the future.

In due course: In a month or two if you are lucky and we don't change our minds.

After the holidays: For goodness sake, don't you realize we are far too busy to bother with you?

Let us know when you are next passing through London: We will make damn sure that you don't catch us napping again.

We very much regret your decision: Thank the Lord for that.

WE

VERY MUCH

REGRET

·········· *your* ··········

DECISION

THANK

THE LORD

= FOR THAT =

We tried to get you on the telephone, but there was no reply: If you catch me out on this, I can always blame my secretary or the telephone exchange.

I am sorry I was out when you called: Didn't you know I had a well-trained secretary?

I would have very much liked: Heaven forfend.

In any other circumstances of course: You must be mad.

In Mr Smith's absence on the Continent: He has no intention of writing to you himself.

We are putting your letter on our files: It is going straight into the wastepaper-basket.

Owing to a previous engagement: I had no intention of accepting.

It is not what the public are demanding at the moment: Quite impossible.

Please do not rest on my opinion alone: I wonder if it can be as bad as I thought.

We will look into this matter: Why on earth did you remind us?

Perhaps next time you are in town, you would telephone my secretary: She is better at thinking up excuses than I am.

I would like to put you in the picture: It is rather dicey, so we had better stick to the same story.

I would like to give your suggestion further consideration: I can't think of an adequate reason for saying 'no' at the moment.

Perhaps you would get in touch with me again after Easter (Whitsun, Christmas, the New Year, in the spring, summer, autumn, or winter): I am just being kind, as I have no intention of seeing you at all.

I would like to discuss the matter with my fellow directors: I don't want to take *all* the blame.

Could you prepare a synopsis?: We'll take a grudging look at it if you are really prepared to go to all this trouble, but it almost certainly won't get you anywhere.

The art of telegram writing is dying out, like that of letter writing. Remember that a good telegram can have much more impact than a letter or a telephone call, particularly if it is at all witty. But never economize on them. The fact that they are so comparatively expensive nowadays means that you should never appear to be counting the number of words. For, as all successful men know, you must always spend money to make money.

Never forget that it is a small world, quite apart from jet aircraft, and that your junior today may be your superior tomorrow. If you part company with anybody, do it on the most amicable terms possible. You never know what is going to happen next in these days of mergers and take-overs. Avoid any form of arrogance and try never to make an enemy, however justified you may feel. Remember the old army song 'I've got my captain working for me now', and that sooner or later you may just as likely pass someone going up as going down. Try not to hate people. It is too exhausting.

The correct use of the telephone, both for incoming and outgoing calls, can affect your popularity and therefore your chances of success to a considerable degree. Nothing is more irritating than to have your personal telephone ring and then hear the secretary at the other end of the line ask you to hang on until your actual caller comes to the telephone. It is not only rude, but also unwise. The suggestion is that his time is more valuable than yours. The reverse is also the case and many a contract has been lost in this way.

Today, there is an increasing habit for people to end the conversation by saying 'Thank you for telephoning'. It is a good trick. It makes you feel that you have gone out of your way to do them a kindness and that they are indebted to you, however trivial the call.

If your own personal telephone rings, always allow it to do so for at least five or ten seconds. Otherwise, it will sound as if you are hanging on to the end of the line in a fever of impatience and anxiety. This breaks all business rules of common sense. Never appear to be in a hurry. Never show any signs of urgency. Try to be as relaxed as Perry Como, however tense the situation. When telephoning for an interview or making a luncheon date, put it off as far ahead as possible. Always pretend to consult your own diary before accepting an invitation over the telephone, even though it is completely blank for a fortnight ahead.

If you know that a conversation is going to be important and complicated, arrange for your secretary to listen on a second line and take the other person's conversation down in shorthand. But let her pick up her receiver at exactly the same moment as yourself, so that there is no revealing little click to disclose your stratagem.

Never shout down the telephone and remember that if there are any imperfections in your voice, they are more likely to be revealed on the telephone than in ordinary conversation.

Never talk longer than necessary. Don't forget that one of the best ways of ending a conversation is by saying that you are wanted on another line.

Never telephone a business acquaintance between a quarter to one and three o'clock. If you do, and he is out, it looks as though you are anxious when you call him the second time. The best time is round about a quarter past three when he is presumably back from what you hope is a good luncheon.

Never telephone after five o'clock on a Friday. He is liable to be leaving earlier than usual for the weekend. Be very chary about telephoning him at home, out of office hours, unless he has specifically given you his private number for this very purpose. Otherwise he may feel that you are taking an unfair advantage of him.

Swearing, down the telephone, or otherwise, is very stupid. It shows that you have no proper vocabulary, not just that you have a choleric disposition. If you cannot emphasize a noun without the use of 'bloody', it means that you are badly educated.

Incidentally, the Irish very seldom use an oath, however much they may call on the Saints. And if you ever tell an Irish story, never use the word 'Begorrah'. No Irishman ever uses it, though he may indeed say 'Begob'.

If you are personally answering a direct telephone call, the simplest reply is 'Yes?' and let the other person announce his identity before you disclose yours. To give your name, or even your number, as advocated by some people, may mean that you cannot easily hedge if you do not wish to speak to your caller. Avoid, if possible, on these occasions, the hackneyed phrase of being 'in conference'. Nobody believes it, particularly when your secretary says it for you.

Worse still is the secretary's phrase 'Oh, he has just gone out', unless it is meant to be a deliberate snub on your behalf. Let her dream up something more original, like 'He has gone to his dentist'. If anyone invites you to call him back, don't do anything so silly. If he really wants to be in touch with you, he will call you back himself and the squeeze is on him.

White lies on the telephone should be as convincing as possible.

Sooner or later, the time will come when you have to learn the mystique of dealing on the telephone with the Press yourself,

WHITE LIES ON THE TELEPHONE should be as CONVINCING AS POSSIBLE

whether or not you employ a P.R.O. or a public relations firm. The first rule is to remember that you can always trust the editor, though not necessarily gossip writers and free lance journalists, who are only too anxious to secure by-lines and play up a newspaper story as fully, even sensationally, as possible. But editors can, we repeat, always be trusted not to break confidences. This does not, however, always apply to one or two hot-stuff City Editors, who can be very awkward.

If, by any chance, the matter is so urgent that you yourself have to telephone, remember that (a) Sunday newspaper staffs are never in the office on Mondays; (b) that Editors' conferences on daily newspapers take place usually between noon and one o'clock, so this is an awkward time; (c) Editors of evening newspapers are particularly busy between eleven o'clock and two.

It is always better to meet the editor personally.

Most of them, however, have so many luncheon engagements that they are likely to be booked days ahead.

Wherever possible, when dealing with newspapers, be as frank as possible. They will appreciate it. But if someone telephones you on behalf of a newspaper, delving into some personal or business affair on which you cannot possibly allow yourself to be quoted, there is only one recourse—the magic, if tiresome phrase, 'No comment'.

You may think you are safe if someone asks you whether you are aware that, for example, your rivals have undercut you on a big business deal and you reply in what you think is a non-committal way 'I must have notice of that question', but there is quite a danger that you will be quoted as saying that you did not deny it. This might not be at all what you meant.

Telephone interviews can often be dangerous. And if you allow a really smart reporter into your home, he may notice things that you had no wish to be revealed.

Remember that if you write a letter to *The Times* it must be exclusive. If you send a duplicate to the *Daily Telegraph* or any other newspaper, and it is printed there as well, you will find that *The Times* has a long memory. It likes its letter columns to be exclusive.

Many big firms employ 'spokesmen' so that when an awkward question is fired at them out of the blue, there is always time to think up an answer while they are consulting you. Another advantage of a spokesman is that what he says is always regarded as less interesting and therefore is given less prominence than if it is said by the head of the firm or a senior partner.

If you can ever give a newspaper a good story which has nothing to do with your own business, do so. They become your friends at once. On such occasions, you get in touch with the news editor—or the night news editor if it is after seven o'clock.

If you have something to report about your own business which is really of national importance, get in touch with the Press Association. Otherwise give it to only one newspaper with the assurance that it is exclusive. You can be sure of far more space being devoted to it than if you give it to several.

Never try to bribe a reporter any more than you would bribe a policeman. It is his job to get the news, however unpalatable.

Never sue a newspaper if you can possibly help it. Never appeal to newspaper proprietors. It will get you nowhere.

Never demand a complete withdrawal unless it is absolutely essential. Persuade the editor to return to the subject in the next issue with a different angle which nevertheless straightens things out as far as possible. In fact, never become unpopular with the Press. The power they wield is immense, particularly if they decide to ignore you totally.

Book critics have easily the highest standard of integrity in Fleet Street, compared with those of the theatre, cinema, sport, and even music critics. They may damn authors to high heaven, but they are never, well practically never, really destructive just for the devil of it. They are by no means all sweetness and light. But they are never so egocentric as certain theatre critics we could name. For one thing, they are, almost without exception, well educated and well-mannered.

You never need fear any injurious remark from either radio or television. On the other hand, they can be immensely useful if you happen to know, or get to know, any of the producers. They are the people who count.

NEVER
BE SARCASTIC
TO ANYONE
·········*whether*·········
IN PUBLIC
or
IN PRIVATE
IT CAN BE
VERY WOUNDING
·········*and will*·········
NEVER BE FORGOTTEN
PARTICULARLY
BY NEWSPAPERMEN

Employ a press-cutting agency, not only for yourself and your business, but also order the clippings of your rivals' activities. There is no law against this and it often provides invaluable information about what they are doing not only at home but also abroad. But perhaps you do so already? It is an invaluable 'private eye'.

If you are not used to making public speeches, go to an expert coach, as the Duke of Bedford did. It is also worthwhile buying *Public Speaking and Chairmanship* by Frederick Mills.

If you ever give evidence in court, look a trifle scared—which you probably will be anyway. The Judge will love you for your appreciation of the majesty of the law. And, of course, try to avoid being hostile in cross-examination, however unpleasant Counsel may be.

Never be sarcastic to anyone, whether in public or in private. It can be very wounding and will never be forgotten, particularly by newspapermen. They have long memories.

If you wish not to be seen, entering or leaving the country on a business or private trip to the Continent, never fly. Go by train, whether it is the Golden Arrow or the Night Ferry. There are too many newshawks at London Airport and none at Victoria Station.

Much of the skill in public relations is to know how to keep out of print, when your activities are hot news. It is even more difficult than getting your name into the newspapers when you want publicity. But both depend upon tact and timing.

Tact is an abbreviation of tacit. More business deals have been lost and more law cases gone adrift through too much talk than for any other reason. Always remember the story of the officer's friend and the soldier servant, and the phrase, 'Call me early, Mother dear, for I'm to be Queen of the May'. It remains the perfect warning about overplaying the hand.

If you earn a reputation as a good mimic or an amusing gossip, you won't go very far.

If you are acting as a third party when introducing a buyer to

IF YOU EARN
A REPUTATION
as a
GOOD MIMIC
or an
AMUSING GOSSIP
YOU WON'T GO
VERY FAR

a seller, make sure that you know the right moment at which to say 'What is there in it for me?' If you leave it too late you will probably be given a warm champagne cocktail for your pains. It has happened before now, and will happen again.

If you are doing any insurance with Lloyd's, tell the whole truth. *Suppressio Veri* is unforgivable and very dangerous. It is the exact opposite, in fact, of the ordinary run of social life, where it is sometimes unforgivable to tell the whole truth and nothing but the truth. The real truth can be very painful.

In conclusion, there is a recent phrase, 'The Establishment', which presumably derives from people being complementary or supernumerary to the Establishment in the military sense of the word. To refer to the Establishment in a derogatory way suggests that you yourself are supernumerary to the powers that be. In other words, you are below the salt, not accepted, without power or authority and therefore frustrated, in fact that you have not 'arrived'—a solemn thought.

British Library Cataloguing in Publication Data
A catalogue record for this book is available
from the British Library

ISBN-13: 978-0-85965-545-3

Cover and book design by Coco Balderrama
Printed by Bell & Bain Ltd. in Great Britain